BROWN NEON

BROWN NEON

RAQUEL GUTIÉRREZ

COFFEE HOUSE PRESS

Minneapolis

2022

Image credits: cover image © ACDash/iStock; adobe bricks, Karlitos Espinosa Miller, and photo of *Spiral Jetty* © Raquel Gutiérrez; *Nature Self-Portrait #14*, 1996 © Laura Aguilar Trust of 2016; *no water under the bridge* © Carol Cheh; *A masked worker fumigates a bracero with DDT at the Hidalgo Processing Center, Texas, while others wait in line* © Leonard Nadel Photographs and Scrapbooks, Archives Center, National Museum of American History, Smithsonian Institution

Excerpts from the work of Jeanne Córdova used by permission.

Coffee House Press books are available to the trade through our primary distributor, Consortium Book Sales & Distribution, cbsd.com or (800) 283-3572. For personal orders, catalogs, or other information, write to info@coffeehousepress.org.

Coffee House Press is a nonprofit literary publishing house. Support from private foundations, corporate giving programs, government programs, and generous individuals helps make the publication of our books possible. We gratefully acknowledge their support in detail in the back of this book.

LIBRARY OF CONGRESS CATALOGING-IN-PUBLICATION DATA

Names: Gutiérrez, Raquel, 1976– author.
Title: Brown neon / Raquel Gutiérrez.
Description: Minneapolis : Coffee House Press, 2022.
Identifiers: LCCN 2021056505 (print) | LCCN 2021056506 (ebook) |
    ISBN 9781566896375 (paperback) | ISBN 9781566896450 (epub)
Subjects: LCGFT: Essays.
Classification: LCC PS3607.U819 B76 2022 (print) | LCC PS3607.U819
    (ebook) | DDC 814/.6—dc23/eng/20211221
LC record available at https://lccn.loc.gov/2021056505
LC ebook record available at https://lccn.loc.gov/2021056506

PRINTED IN THE UNITED STATES OF AMERICA

29 28 27 26 25 24 23 22   1 2 3 4 5 6 7 8

For my three fathers
José Javier Olvera Gutiérrez
Jeanne Córdova
Ignacio "Nacho" Nava

It was the strangest feeling. Like bones melting.
Like sun shining through the darkness of your eyelids.

—"THE MOTHS," HELENA MARIA VIRAMONTES

Table of Contents

BROWN NEON

SECTION I

LLORANDO POR TU AMOR

On Making Butch Family:
An Intertextual Dialogue

2015 | The battery light shines red on my dashboard, a warning jolting me out of an obsessive sing-along. I am alone in my car again, repeating the hook of "Lovin', Touchin', Squeezin'," as a way to offset the numbness that comes with the unremarkable parts of a road trip in progress. On the highway I'm just another heavy heart lifted by song, imagining loved ones shrinking in the distance with each stolen glance at the rearview mirror.

My reptilian brain is low on dopamine again. It wants its queer family. It wants to hit Steve Perry–high notes next time it does karaoke. It wants to be on to the next occasion.

The possibility of my car breaking down and preventing me from orchestrating the next occasion sends a chill. My car has never broken down before and certainly not in the big, bad, scary desert.

I travel west on the 10 heading back to Los Angeles, trudging through 103 degrees of Arizona's unsparing desert heat. As soon as I touch down in Quartzsite, one of the last towns near the state line, I go for my car owner's manual. Just how screwed could I possibly be with three hundred miles still to go?

The electrical system is on the verge of shutting down. I decide that if I am going to break down, I want to do it in a blue state. I have more than twenty miles to go before I hit Blythe, California. I get back in my car, take a deep breath, roll down the windows, and head west. To Blythe.

Blythe is a place I have newly begun to appreciate as the last bastion of chill brown Califas. I don't want to be an irredeemably spoiled Californian brat and call bad vibes, but it was 2016 and the wound of SB 1070 was still fresh. The "show-me-your-papers" law was first a bill that included provisions that gave law enforcement the power to determine anyone's immigration status during any lawful stop. SB 1070 also pushed for the requirement for all "alien" noncitizens to carry "registration documents." Undocumented people couldn't seek employment. Arguably the worst were the warrantless arrests. Folks could be arrested for just being suspected of being undocumented. If we didn't see the seeds of fascism being planted in this 2010 series of planned violences, then we weren't looking hard enough. How, in 2010, could we not know that people we knew (or knew of) were already being disappeared?

This has been the way political structures permeate the sweeping views of Arizona's stunning terrains. State power is always present in the natural environment. But it's not confined solely to Arizona, just as every state in the union claims a flower as its own. This occurs to me as I pass the *Welcome to California* sign. I haven't seen the golden poppies that adorn the sign but know they bloom year-round. It is the poet's job to make you fall in love with the idea of state flowers—its promise of a shared identity built around a regional flower that relies more on bee pollination than water. Who could be unmoved by such a seduction?

I grew up seeing those beguiling orange poppies while making the drive between California's deserts. As a kid, I was taken to see members of my mother's family eking out lives as casino mechanics and shopowners in Las Vegas and Boulder City, Nevada. Or we would take family vacations in Lake Havasu or Bullhead City in Arizona. There were always golden fields ablaze with these funny-named flowers. It was the homonym for the name my sister and I used to address our father—papí. Our father. He was our first, intrepid navigator through these southwestern desert roads in hardy vehicles, like our plushed-out Econoline van, carpeted and upholstered in cobalt blue and replete with antenna television.

I see the familiar date palms in the distance. This is how I self-soothe while anticipating the imminent moment of vehicular collapse. I pray that we (my car and I are one) will make it there in one piece.

Just as I cross the Arizona-California state line checkpoint, I rev the engine and shift to hit seventy-five miles per hour before the car begins to shut down on me. Blythe: next four exits. I just need the first one. The lights on the odometer begin to flash, the digital clock flicks all zeros and the stereo pops through my speakers. It feels a little *Back to the Future,* and my improvised DeLorean is tearing through the desert's space-time continuum. The first exit finally appears and I coast across lanes and make my first "California Stop" since high school in order to peter out in front of a tractor tow lot. I'm good. It's not a miracle by any means, but I made land art with that descent.

I call for roadside assistance, check that my phone is charged and that I still have two big bottles of water to get me through the next couple of hours. A sigh of relief that I've been careful with my recent expenditures as I have just enough credit limit to pay for whatever damages my car is about to cost me. I thank Tucson for being so cheap. And I'm glad my lover and son are not in my car.

Parting was hard.

I get out of the car, light a cigarette, and take in my surroundings. I had places to be but now time splits open for me. I'm stuck—in my career, in my relationship—and now en route back to the couch I surfed in Los Angeles County when all I wanted was to be in Tucson. But I don't have a community there with couches to choose from. Trucks and tumbleweed and the hum of the interstate a few yards away—the sturdy stuff that can occupy the same space as the desert without totally melting. I'm melting. I used to be sturdy but now I melt. And between huffs of nicotine smoke and rivulets of sweat forming on the small of my back, I feel myself seesawing between sturdy and molten in the desert heat. The tow truck and technician finally come and, after the last call with the third auto shop, I know there is no way I'm going to Los Angeles anytime soon.

The desert isn't ready to let go. This is just the first battle in the video game called *Someone in Tucson Hearts Me,* named after the threadbare yellow vintage T-shirt I had bought even though it was an extra small. The desert and I have only just begun.

In the summer of 2015 my young adopted son returned home from San Francisco and threw a party for me. Due to the cancer, I couldn't throw a party, get the beer, barbecue and girls together. I could only appear, dressed dapperly, walk haltingly around the poolside with my mermaid-headed cane. I wanted to give away to other

masculine-of-center younger women thousands of dollars'
worth of almost-unworn men's shirts and pants. It was
butch bonding.

Big Poppa was a writer.[1] She was on the heels of her memoir,
When We Were Outlaws, winning a Lambda Literary Award
four years before she died. The section above is from an essay
she tried to pen about our relationship, but the cancer in her
cerebellum made it hard to finish. I read it from time to time
when I start to forget what Big Poppa sounded like; when I
forget what I might have meant to her. Her illness is why I'm
so desperate to get back to Los Angeles to see Big Poppa, who
was finally starting to receive visitors after an intensely tax-
ing round of chemotherapy. I'm traveling back from Tucson
just a few weeks after having moved back to Los Angeles from
the Bay Area. I had been living out of boxes and tote bags prior
to this break down in Blythe. Desire pulled in so many directions—ending relationships, starting relationships, doing art
full-time. This plus the needful act of performing some kind of
discernible adulthood for my parents and their concern for my
negative net worth. It was an anarchy of coping with so much
change afoot, and I had yet to get on Big Poppa's calendar.

I had last seen her in early July to coordinate and host
her big butch clothing swap and early birthday party. Big
Poppa—or Jeanne, as I had known her before our intimacy—
wanted to see the clothes that hung on her now-thin frame
go to the younger butches in our lesbian Los Angeles world.

---

1. The depth of impact Jeanne Córdova had on lesbian culture and human
rights activism will continue to be measured for decades to come, but to me
she is a child of southern California, of multiple lives and deaths, vision and
reinvention. I urge you to read *When We Were Outlaws* to begin to understand
the mission of her life.

That meant I was tasked with going into Jeanne's closets and pulling out custom-made suits, brand-name blue jeans, finely tailored shirts with French cuffs, polos, and slacks, and creating a temporary clothing post. And I was more than happy to accommodate all of Big Poppa's wishes—no whim was too big or small. This was my way of honoring her and doing so in the comfort of her home. Jeanne and her spouse of twenty-six years, Lynn, lived in a beautiful Mediterranean-style house in the hills of Los Feliz, a neighborhood near Griffith Park and the Hollywood studios. Many houses in these famous hills are anything but ordinary. This was the Farrell House, designed by Frank Lloyd Wright Jr. in 1926. It was a glorious place that felt like a bit of Hearst Castle had chipped away and fallen into this corner of Los Angeles, an elegant retreat for Big Poppa to hold court, where she could both rest and be as convivial as she was kingly.

We had become close five years earlier, in 2010, our relationship sealed after I played "Jeanne Córdova" in a short play Big Poppa wrote based on excerpts from *When We Were Outlaws*. Big Poppa had earlier come to know my performance work with the ensemble Butchlalis De Panochtitlan. She and Lynn would come to see our original performance art compositions illustrating different brown butch histories lodged in the lore of the Los Angeles neighborhoods the four of us Butchlalis either grew up in, or near, or currently lived in. The short play Big Poppa wrote would become the cornerstone of her Los Angeles book party for *When We Were Outlaws*. I loved the idea of forgoing a reading and staging lesbian history onstage. Big Poppa enjoyed my portrayal of a youthful, brash, blustering journalist and free-loving seducer she had created with her younger protagonized self, Young Córdova. My performance was received so well that lesbians who came of age politically with Big Poppa called me "Young Córdova" for several years after. The experience pleased Big Poppa so much, and the love and affection that grew between us was so palpable that, like a lover chasing another, she declared to me that she would be my father. And I, her son. We were a dying breed, she said. Aside from the hard fact that she actually *was* dying, Big Poppa was a dapper butch dandy—someone who fought long and hard to own that identity, only to live out her last days seeing it carted off to the elephant graveyard of queer self-determination. The gender binary was losing its luster as a desirable barometer for queer gender, which meant that *butch* was falling in and out of fashion, a complicated monolith awaiting its meteor or sanctuary. Butch was often that category of queer ontology that had to be periodically rescued from the bin of bad punchlines. Queer sociability was slowly pulling the curtain back on what felt like the diminished relationship to an identity Big Poppa and I shared. I wanted to age gracefully in the face of perceived disappearance. Big Poppa was actually disappearing though. The butchness between us was ultimately a feeling of recognition that granted us language and confidence despite the generation between us. It was a quotidian inspiration—and not everyone gets that in their daily lives. It's why Big Poppa proudly snapped her cufflinks into place every day she had left with us.

The elaborations that moved beyond butch as a category didn't stop me from trying to live each day with similar aplomb either, but it was also the cancer that had viciously followed her for the last decade that made our bond that much more immediate and necessary. My reavowal of a butch identity felt like re-enlistment—I was following Big Poppa into war as her loyal subordinate. There was so much I wanted to know and experience through Big Poppa's five senses, and I felt the time ticking away from us. I wanted to be who she saw. But I was still cautious with Big Poppa—her declaration of butch fatherhood meant a lot to me, but as an adult child of an alcoholic father I was so used to being disappointed that I didn't want to set my heart on anything with anyone new. Anything by way of love? Acceptance? Recognition? Validation? It was my cautiousness that had always been the cornerstone of self-sabotage as far as my relationships went. I struggled to make them last. These tools were the things that my own father could not provide me when I was a child and teenager. And each year the distance between us widened—he, a Mexican immigrant who had a penchant for staying out late, philandering, and making bad economic decisions that would impact his family. He, a Mexican man who for one reason or another couldn't remember the names of his grandparents whenever I asked him about our family. It wasn't until I learned that my grandmother had birthed her firstborn son out of wedlock that I understood the murky connection to our larger family tree in Mexico. My dad tried to instill a bond the best way he could, by talking about the outstanding things of his hometown, Pachuca. Whether it was his drunken exaltation of Reloj Monumental, the watch tower built to commemorate the Mexican revolution, or of Club de Fútbol Pachuca, one of the oldest soccer teams in modern-day Mexico, my dad found ways to keep his Mexico alive in a country that tried to cannibalize him. Yet, in the space of our home it was easier for me to adopt more of my mother's Salvadoranness, even though I would travel to Mexico more often, free of any fear about what my queer gender might attract in terms of violent attention. My queerness never bothered my Mexican dad. It was the fact that I was born in Los Angeles, had a handful of college degrees, and yet still couldn't muster a net worth he could be proud of. He couldn't make sense out of me, unable to be self-made in the way he had to be out of necessity first, and then out of the will to feed the greed that follows when success is achieved. Me—a struggling artist-convener-writer and what? A professional queer? What is it that I actually do?

I was afraid of becoming a known figure in activist Chicanoville because I mostly grew up in white culture with my white Irish mother. I wasn't working class in the age that identified most Latinas as such, afraid I didn't have the street credentials, that I had only a Mexican father to teach me.

I devoted myself to Jeanne. We saw the traces of Mexicanidad in one another in ways that were important to us—that we had the troubled marks upon us thanks to our complicated Mexican fathers, who would work themselves to death not in the fields but in maintaining the wealth they had won against the odds.

Big Poppa. My Big Poppa.

Our relationship meant that I was in charge of inviting the assortment of butches from L.A.'s queer and lesbian communities to Big Poppa's swath of paradise. And they came—a young brown butch from Riverside, a professor butch from Echo Park, a handful of older butches from Big Poppa's West Hollywood days, a few hipster butches, and a couple of artist butches, too. They came and tried stuff on but only about half of the clothing swap attendees went home with a number of items. Big Poppa had been fairly robust in size, and wheelbarrows full of fine duds were left on the tables and hangers. We both lamented that I wouldn't be able to benefit from her generous offering since I wore a men's medium in shirts and had a thirty-three-inch waist. My ample bosom and big mouth had fooled Big Poppa into thinking I was much larger, but I'm actually just petite but portly.[2]

We were more than halfway through the afternoon barbecue gathering when Caleb[3] strolled in with a princely bottle of bourbon in hands that resembled little league baseball mitts. He arrived confidently, the only visually pronounced trans guy in the room. His usually unkempt beard was trimmed and his mustache was now shaped handsomely, accentuating the angles in his jawbone and framing his bright white awkward smile as he came into a party space with all lesbian eyes on him. I wasn't the only one dazzled by how well put together he looked—how comfortable he seemed in his body—leaner, stronger, and anchored in dark denim and a sense of inner calm. People notice that stuff. It's what makes us fall in love.

The only trans guy who came was Caleb. He got a whole wardrobe for his first-in-the-family try at graduate school. His valet? The party-planner and my son, Raquel. Being a proper Chicano butch, she fussed over him, buttoning unknown buttons, straightening a lapel, tucking in fine shirts.

I encouraged Caleb to try on a couple of the long sleeve button-ups that hung in excess on the makeshift clothing rack I had jimmied between two branches of a white alder tree in front of the pool house. The first shirt he tried on, a baby-blue gingham long-sleeve, fit his barrel chest and short,

---

2. I suppose I have to cite Zach Galifianakis in his portrayal of Chip Baskets for the apt description of those with my body type.

3. Not his real name.

thickset arms perfectly. I ooh'ed and ahh'ed every time one of Jeanne's tailored shirts hugged his body as though they were tailored just for him. What were the chances? Each shirt— the pink oxford, the navy stripe, and the madras checks in monochromatic neutrals—wrapped around his body with ease and elegance. He was no longer the nervous baby butch dyke in punk, patched denim jackets with cut-off sleeves and dilapidated combat boots. He was no longer the homeless baby butch dyke kicked out of a religious home, disowned by a homophobic Jehovah's Witness family of cannery workers. He was no longer the baby butch dyke living out of a car outside the orchards of Riverside or sleeping in tents following the Occupy movement up to Oakland and back down Interstate 5. He was our young man now. And a part of me felt the pang of losing the feral quality of his iconoclastic youth as I saw Caleb transition into a legible adulthood by way of a respectable wardrobe. His maturation meant I had to double down on my own. But I would be damned if Caleb wasn't the best dressed guy in the graduate program he was due to leave for in a month.

I beamed with pride.

But in that moment Big Poppa lacked the jubilance I was emanating. She had a cloudy look about her that I had trouble reading. Was this a well-worn panic playing out before me, I wondered. Was there a sudden rupture in familiarity? Was this a case of losing butches to unexamined male privilege? I was more anxious about Caleb treading the troubling waters of class mobility once he left Southern California, but maybe I was alone in that concern. Was I misreading the furrowed brows on the faces of the other butch elders? I was reminded of Cherríe L. Moraga's reprimand in a 2009 essay called "Still Loving in the (Still) War Years/2009: On Keeping Queer

Queer." Moraga polarized queer audiences with her candid take on the fear she had of lesbians abandoning feminism to assume commodified masculine identities as brown trans men. But aren't all of our identities imbricated by the sticky annals of empire and capitalism? Hasn't that identification with accumulation burdened us all to arrive to legibility through wealth and structural platforms?

It is these moments that seize me with my own fear. These are the particularities that clarify the ways in which we need each other, how we might midwife for one another the image we form of ourselves. These are the moments that have shown the limits of community, much like the limits of families of origin, in that we are always some reflexive extension of someone else and thus captive to their expectations. And that there's something about these expectations that leave the individual other ontologically exhausted.

I tuned out the noise but not the history that grounded Moraga's sentiment. I was tired of pitting butch dykes against trans men in some imaginary gladiator arena that haunted the dreams of butch elders. Big Poppa fought for the right to wear her custom-tailored suits in a time that marked the butch as a patsy for patriarchy. Now her queer grandchildren were fighting for the right to transition genders or to do away with the binary altogether. And I was going to hold open the portal that allowed for the old-school butch lesbian camaraderie and the new school in gender self-determination to coexist and cross-pollinate.

There would be no lesbian activism on the West Coast without Big Poppa, who played a huge role as organizer and commentator. She was part of the collective that organized the West Coast Lesbian Feminist Conference, the first ever convergence of its kind in 1973. Even then, in that political and cultural milieu, being a butch lesbian was suspect, and I was well aware of how much Big Poppa suffered in keeping that major part of her identity at bay for the comfort of other lesbian kin and comrades who held misgivings about anything remotely butch.

Big Poppa wasn't the first person to convey how important my butch identity was. I had had enough random bar encounters with a range of queers telling me unprovoked that I was a unicorn, how fleeting and unique I was because "all of the real butches" were transitioning. This was queer culture for a good chunk of the early aughts, when butches and femmes began to decouple. Like the dollar to the gold standard, we were finally determining our own currency in the new century. By the time I got to New York for grad school in 2003, everyone around me had not quite had enough with binaries even as gender was getting another pass through the meaning-making machines of liberal East Coast colleges, or a few years later through social media technologies like Tumblr. We found new ways beyond the bar to connect. Our desires for recognition were similar. We started building language together, agreeing to the terms and acknowledging the harms from there within. But moving from Chicana lesbian Los Angeles to queer futures New York meant inhabiting new social circles with tier-1 queers of color who had graduated to new ontological vocabularies informed by queer theory.

I was excited by the coupling of queerness to theory, but I had been a commuter student trying to make each credit count for my journalism major at a state university in the San Fernando Valley of Southern California. I couldn't imagine new forms of desire because butch-femme coupling had been my lesbian norm, although I likely would have transitioned myself if I had grown up in an environment that valued mental health and had access to culturally sensitive mental health specialists. But that wasn't available for me. Good healthcare is hard to come by and I was scared to amass more debt. I also balked at therapy. When I got back to Los Angeles in 2005, I paid five dollars for sliding-scale therapy with a salty Bostonian logging her hours at the Gay and Lesbian Center in Hollywood, in an office decorated with Red Sox paraphernalia. Her best advice was to break up with the person I was dating at that time. Throughout my twenties, I had been cautioned to remain queer and resist whatever spoils came with being a warrior for mainstream and binaristic masculinity. In hindsight, as if in the Cher Horowitz register, it was another battle of identity—legibility against ambiguity. Who would nurse me back to health if I got top surgery? I learned to be comfortable not with my body but with always being at odds with it. The situational incongruence was the price of being queer.

In my mind, I have been too plenty, too eager to offer myself, and so of course I was delighted for the attention from Big Poppa. Yet, I felt the burden of that affirmation and what it meant to respond with assurance to her that this was my path, hoping to remain vigilant against casting my own monolithic mold.

Maybe the term "butch" will, like the dinosaurs, become extinct this year. Women who see ourselves as women yet keep our masculine ways, thoughts, dress, and body language will always be a staple of lesbian life. Like I feel silly on this super-hot day sitting here in sleeveless . . . err . . . ok . . . blouse. That feeling won't change with time, though the term might.

I soul-coughed back into the here-and-now and it was still a gorgeous mid-July day with temperate heat and the sunrays dancing with the epitome of cool, Southern California mellow. I made myself remember that Big Poppa was lounging topless in her pool, glistening with a sexy insouciance, smoking her favorite brand and remaining faithful to the way she had lived all the days leading up to that moment. She was among a set of younger, awed dykes who brimmed with curiosity, asking her what it was like to push against the violent currents of a time before they all existed. I made myself remember the feeling of gratitude at being the nearing-middle-age butch who mans the barbecue pit, turning the browning chicken and rare skirt steak shish-kebabs, reveling in my own contentment with being able to share Big Poppa with my friends and peers and let them bear witness to our parent-child relationship. I knew that Big Poppa had a political capaciousness about her that made it possible to understand and embrace where transgender identities and material realities stand along the spectrum of lesbian and queer ways of being. She pushed back against transphobic radical lesbian feminists (her peers and friends in some cases) who wanted to ban trans women from feminist space and discourse. If I lived with the same specter of mortality that she lived with in those days, it would certainly saturate my fantasies of wanting to leave behind a strong butch genealogy. To leave a manual of my experiences as a blueprint for fighting every shade of misogyny. A code of ethics for younger trans masculine queers and butches to abide by while walking the earthly plane. Things happen so quickly that we're all cautioned to put our affairs in order when it's time for the final transition. But to name how we inherited our politics feels important in the here and now, while we can still enjoy one another.

And Caleb, who embodied the blurring between butchness and transness, all the while holding a strong presence in my intimate relational making, complicated that desire, spurring me to stretch myself beyond what suddenly felt like comfort.

I kept myself busy to keep that tension light and productive.

I focused on being a good Party Dad—that is, serving the perfectly grilled animal protein and salads, and making sure the beers, hard seltzers, and sodas were chilled and filled. It was time to bring the red velvet birthday cake from the kitchen to the backyard. This event summoned everyone at the party to stop whatever they were doing and get ready to sing hard and loud.

I would realize later that this would be the last time I'd sing "Happy Birthday" to Big Poppa.

There is a photograph from this gathering that shows me from the shoulders up, arms outstretched, holding the cake while Big Poppa's eyes sparkle with effortless butch charm at the tasteful display of lit birthday cake candles. She blows them out while flanked by Lynn and a few younger butch and femme dykes who came out to pay tribute—younger members of our community who I hoped would one day go on to tell the story of Big Poppa's last birthday party.

I needed to put my hope into Caleb that afternoon. And I needed to quell Big Poppa's anxiety about whether or not I would be next to transition. I saw how these worrisome pangs tumbled out; her agitation that none of the other brown butches in our midst would inherit her sartorial bearings—the material evidence that bolstered her confident swagger for the last three decades—became visible that afternoon. Big Poppa wanted Caleb to stay butch, and because I wanted to keep the family happy, I would tell her that he still identified that way—

the stick-and-poke DYKE tattoo on his left shoulder proved the point—but that he needed, for his own sense of self-making and ultimately sanity, to flatten his chest, deepen his voice, and connect with a center that had eluded him for the twenty-some years of his previous existence.

Yet, there were moments where Big Poppa would surprise me during our conversations about transitioning and "remaining" butch, as if the two were categories and not spaces we could walk in and out of in a given situational context. "My doctor put me on testosterone," she would tell me matter-of-factly over chain-smoked menthol cigarettes and her second Diet Coke. "I loved it. But I was afraid that I did."

> *They are now changing the definition of "butch" to fit more neatly into the present lexicon of trans. They say that "butch" is now a trans term that refers to a masculine woman. I'm glad masculine is no longer necessarily a bad word like it was in the lesbian feminist 70s and 80s. I had to hide my butchness back then, not that friends say, they were fooled one iota. Now we butches are seen as the perhaps last bulwark of sisterhood. Ain't that strange?*

Big Poppa, my big poppa, Caleb's conceptual butch grandparent, a choosing I was facilitating, maybe didn't in that moment understand that Caleb was both whom and where I was moving toward. I steeled myself, knowing that I would need him as her illness promised to progress intensely and swiftly in the coming months. I needed them both. I needed Big Poppa as my queer butch dad because she gave me a sense of where I came from, and she helped me understand that I make sense as I am. Keeping superhumanly busy was my way of coping with the reality too painful to articulate for all of us who knew this would be our last summer with Big Poppa. But I knew I couldn't stay busy forever.

Jeanne—Big Poppa—was whom I had emerged from, as if I were Athena springing from Zeus's head. Zeus was dying though, and our wise Caleb was taking flight soon, into the desert, wearing his father's father's clothes on his back, and we, the earthbound, certain that his wings weren't fixed by wax but by something more ferociously real. We had his back now, and we were preparing ourselves for when he left, needing to keep his back turned on the two of us—his feet moving forward to the place where our love had propelled him, our blessing. Our curse. Big Poppa was bound for a place where she wouldn't need her body anymore, as her pain would no longer contain her. Caleb was bound for the desert.

And I would soon follow.

———

I was feeling closer to Caleb in the days leading up to Big Poppa's community birthday bash. He had been keeping me company throughout the week while I house-sat in my high school best friend, Valentina, and her husband Josh's sweet, seventies-era, modern A-frame in Mount Washington. I was there seeking refuge in my hometown from a Bay Area breakup that was taking its toll on me in the currency of guilt and gutlessness. Back in March, when I thought everything in my life was fairly sedentary and secure, Valentina asked if I would watch her dog and cat and water the succulents while she and Josh and their three-year-old, Ari, traveled to see Josh's family in Michigan. Her trip fell right in the middle of summer, and with a full-time job in one of the biggest arts institutions in San Francisco, I really had no way to do it. But then I got laid off a week after she had asked me, and I knew I didn't want to spend my birthday at another summertime pre–Dyke March picnic at Dolores Park, which had become a customary ritual and one I was growing resentful of as I needed a break from queer whiteness.

"I'll bake you any cake you want," Lila said the previous year when I protested that, as a Stonewall baby, I had spent too many birthdays in Dolores Park during Gay Pride weekend in San Francisco and wanted to go on a trip, maybe just this once. But I relented because Lila loved the "Gay Christmas" that San Francisco offered its local, national, and international LGBTQQIAA community once a year. And I had been the type to just let things happen to me.

I called Valentina and told her I could be in Los Angeles for three weeks to house-sit. I told Lila by phone that it would be my writing retreat and the best birthday gift I could give myself after enduring a most unceremonious layoff earlier that day. It was the second day of Lila's three-week-long stay in Wyoming. She was there to tend to her father's second knee replacement surgery when I told her that I had lost my job. I would be home alone for the next three weeks and had thirty days before I would close out my program manager position. There wasn't anything else she could tell me in that moment except what I wanted and needed to hear: do what your heart needs to heal.

Seven weeks after this conversation, Lila and I ended our relationship.

Caleb had first presented himself to me three years earlier as a community organizer who wanted to bring queer performance art to the part of Riverside he called home. He had a different queer mode of identifying himself—he aligned himself with brown and Black feminists committed to ending systemic and gender violence and loathing toward themselves and one another. He barely scraped by on his part-time job at Planned Parenthood while agitating against the clumsy ally politics of the dominantly white anarchist space in downtown Riverside. He invited me to present some of my performance work to his friends and peers inside the walls of Tikal, the Guatemalan bakery near the University of California, Riverside.

To say I was charmed from the jump would be an understatement.

It was three months after my bakery performance (where I poked and prodded the feedback output of an electric guitar that Caleb had secured for me) when I next heard from Caleb in Los Angeles. He drove out to see me in Pico-Union, west of downtown Los Angeles, to pick my brain about pursuing an advanced degree in Performance Studies, a degree I had obtained almost a decade prior to this meeting.

The meeting was supposed to be easy and uncomplicated—the most I would say is how much New York had changed in ten years and how competitive that program had become. I would push back on grad school and convey as best as I could the ways in which the institution beats the rasquache out of us. But it wasn't uncomplicated. This meeting became a pivot point in our relationship. Caleb, who at this time had a different name not of his choosing, blurted out that he had been living in his car for six months.

He came home with me that night. I had a quick house meeting with my one roommate and her girlfriend, who didn't live with us but didn't *not* live with us either. They both agreed that Caleb should be with us where he was safe. He lived on our couch for two months, and when he found a full-time job, we turned the office into his new bedroom and he became our third roommate, which was good because he had already become my child.

Now Caleb was two weeks away from leaving Los Angeles for Tucson. I found myself simultaneously asking if he was sure he was ready to leave behind a steady, well-paid position with benefits, and rooting for him as he knocked out the last days of his stressful and demanding job as a patient advocate at the only low-income transgender health clinic in South Central Los Angeles. He did that nonprofit work during the day and was also an active volunteer corps member for the new space for cutting-edge performance and visual art situated in Chinatown. He had come a long way toward finding a meaningful foothold in the communities that mattered most to him during the short time we had known each other.

Some nights Caleb would come up to Valentina and Josh's mountain house to smoke cigarettes on the patio and process his intensely religious upbringing and subsequent disownment when his queerness became too hard to hide from his aunt and uncle, leaders in their local Jehovah's Witness chapter. In turn, he would nod his head as I broke down the reasons why my relationship didn't work after five years of trying, mainly that, while I wanted Lila to pursue her medical school dreams, I knew I couldn't follow her into another potential decade of nonchalantly letting things happen to me. Going with a flow that didn't belong to me had begun to weigh me down. His eyes widened as though he were hearing a cautionary tale of failed adulthood. Other nights he would come over to partake in his Xanax stash or my Ativan stash, drink beers, and fall asleep after roaring along to the bloody battle scenes in *Braveheart* and

Gladiator. We were biding our time with these two-man bachelor parties, for we both knew the grains in the hourglass were quickly moving away from us. The only difference between us was that my body was decomposing faster than his.

We would head to Tucson when he finished his clinic work the first week in August—to sweat it out together during the hottest time of the year.

As the departure date neared, I began to panic.

————

The end of the summer saw me back in Los Angeles after dropping Caleb off in Tucson to be in his new habitat. I was on to another house-sitting gig, alone and bereft in Silver Lake. I was unemployed and trying to shake off the depression I felt setting in after returning to a new Los Angeles reality that still seemed so foreign to me. A new sheen of wealth had appeared over the neighborhoods where I had lived in my early twenties. Silver Lake felt so alienating as everyone was thinner, whiter, and more open about striking gold in one of the city's many cultural industries. Cultural workers flipped houses on the side. I was spiraling into an abyss, waiting to see who would climb down after me.

I went to see Big Poppa before the blues became more than just a vestigial function. She was thinner this time around and her mobility was beginning to wane. She sat me down, handed me a can of diet cream soda, and lit one of the many menthol cigarettes I would bum that afternoon.

"So are you sure you're not seeing anybody?" Big Poppa cocked her head at me, a smile slowly unfolding. "I just can't believe that you're really only focusing on your writing."

"You got me, Big Poppa. There's nowhere else to run," I joked between puffs.

I told Big Poppa about *her*—how we met ten years ago and reconnected recently; how we left our white partners to be with one another because that sense of lost familial connection could still be salvaged if we walked one step at a time in each other's direction. I told Big Poppa I wanted to spend what remained of my days with her even if the possibility of being physically together seemed realities away. I told Big Poppa that this was the hardest thing I could do—be with a femme who left a perfectly well-formed and lived life with another—and that I—a pauper, essentially—wouldn't do it any other way.

Big Poppa just kept repeating "Gee . . . whiz," like we were a panel in some queer Archie comic and I had finally chosen Veronica over Betty. I was disarmed by her surprise, as if she were entering her own memory-laden reverie of dyke drama. She was caught up in my conundrum, but I also knew it was the cancer making Big Poppa stammer out the words she wanted to say.

"Did I ever tell you about . . ." Big Poppa finally piped up though her voice trailed off, her bushy salt and pepper eyebrows raised as she turned her eyes toward the window where the light of the magic hour was softly gleaming.

"What was that Big Poppa?" I felt my face flush as I asked her to repeat herself, looking in the same direction that she was. I shifted uncomfortably in my chair. I'm not sure if it was the intimacy we had created between us that was shaking me, or my continued doubt of being able to stand by my admission of ache and desire for fear of losing Big Poppa's love and recognition. But here she was, unable to articulate that reassurance I struggled to receive. I don't know if it was the disease or just the years of naming desire, left and right, like we were marching toward freedom that left us mute with exhaustion the rest of that afternoon.

———————

Big Poppa met Sandy the day after Christmas. I brought Sandy into the musty-yet-magisterial bedroom that had become the medical unit-cum-social hub in Jeanne and Lynn's home. A Christmas tree stood in the corner of the room and CNN was muted on the big-screen television. Big Poppa couldn't walk anymore. The cancer had completely settled into the folds of her brilliant brain. In the days leading up to Sandy's visit, I would lie next to Big Poppa and watch *Vikings,* her new favorite show. This afternoon Sandy sat closest to Jeanne by her bedside, holding both her hands. I went and laid down next to Big Poppa, an ashtray between us, her hand making its way to the top of my head where she patted it awkwardly, a cigarette barely hanging on between her index and middle fingers. She and Sandy talked for about an hour, bonding over their Tejano roots, Big Poppa touching on her own Sephardic Jewish identity.

> *The pieces finally clicked and I don't remember how we left Santa Fe. The pieces, his over-emphasis on the girls that we must all finish college, the broken nose-bump on his nose, the same on Grandma Estella Hinojosa Córdova, the piñatas, my long talk with prima Professor Madga Hinosa from Dallas, my father's early death-bed conversion from nothing to Catholicism, his Latin parents' life of no religion, Grandpa's belief in voodoo figures. My part life as a Sephardic Jew began to make sense.*

Sandy was charmed by Jeanne's tales of lesbian historical dramas, gossip, and failed separatist utopian fantasies. I begged Big Poppa to tell Sandy an abridged version of the story of a drunken Kate Millett coming out to address a group of ornery lesbians at the 1973 West Coast Lesbian Conference at UCLA.

I longed for her final blessing.

"I didn't think I was going to, but I really like her," Big Poppa said to me between her burdened breathing and the next drag of her menthol. Sandy had left the room to use the bathroom down the hall. "But," she started, her eyes fixed upon me, so unwavering and glossy that I braced myself for what I hoped would be what I needed to hear, knowing that this would be one of our last visits.

"You've got a lot of growing up to do."

A Butch in the Desert

2016 | Ten days into the new year and Big Poppa was gone. The last time I saw her she was in a handsome, silk, slate-blue bathrobe, watching CNN hosts speculate on the 2016 election still nearly a year out.

That was five days ago.

Big Poppa had been on her side of the bed, smoking in her bedroom inside a house in the beautiful Mediterranean-inspired Los Feliz hillside neighborhood, where she had always longed to live. She had been a nanny in her UCLA days for Quintana Roo Dunne, the adopted daughter of Joan Didion and John Gregory Dunne, perhaps the most read West Coast literary figures of the twentieth century. The family lived in Los Feliz, and the couple were Big Poppa's introduction to the life of the writer, the younger Córdova seeing the way two writers could think and write interdependently, passing in the hallway without speaking, their cigarettes on the verge of breaking ash. That is what she had always wanted.

Today I can't help but fixate on whether or not Big Poppa died thinking Hillary Clinton would ease into office. She looked so strong the last time I saw her that I thought we would get another two or three months to confidently speculate on the future of the country, a future that didn't include her.

I pushed the blankets away, my body an oven, and sat up in bed. It was an unusually chilly January morning in southeast Los Angeles, the sound of the barrio softly booming with banda, a sign of late Saturday night spilling into the early Sunday haze of hangover. The noise was layered by my phone vibrating with the news of her death. My neighbors would be heading to church soon and I was still lying under several layers of mismatched blankets; the walls in my room were cold to the touch. I felt the blood rush to my head. My mouth, dry. And my heart, of course, was pounding on the door of my chest.

Oh, Jeanne.

I looked at my phone and automatically dialed Sandy's number.

Sandy was in Austin when I called, ending a conference weekend over a big brunch with a much beloved mentor. She kept sending me to voicemail. I spiraled into the mouth of new grief. I texted, *Jeanne died,* and she finally picked up.

I'm so sorry, Gata.

I hung up the phone. She did her best to comfort me from the noisy foyer of a hopping brunch spot in downtown. I wanted her words to soothe before the maelstrom of terrifying sadness came for me.

She was who I had brought home to Big Poppa, who had posed with Big Poppa in a few photos I knew I had to snap. Big Poppa, whose eyes instinctively sparked at being cradled by Sandy's ample femme curves, and now Big Poppa was gone. All the blessings were starting to mix—on my behalf, Jeanne had loved Sandy, an accomplished, gorgeous, Chicana femme with a beautiful mind to match. But Big Poppa's words had been haunting me. Would I be on equal footing with Sandy in Big Poppa's eyes? Was I stable and healthy enough to enter into an adult relationship with someone who had a career while I floundered on my mother's couch? Why was stable adulthood hard for me to inhabit? Could adulthood be legible in other ways? Big Poppa had left this earthly plane, her body in pain, leaving me to figure out what it meant to be a grown butch on the precipice of forty. Would I ever make her proud?

Before the cancer kept Big Poppa bedridden, she and I would ride around town, grabbing coffee, sitting around the park benches in Little Tokyo, and shopping for boots and leather jackets, shooting the good shit between us, butch dad and butch son. Our identification with masculinity playfully threaded over language. Jeanne would never be my mom, nor I her daughter. Our butchness was so ingrained in our queer bodies that we read as ladies only to a world that didn't really matter to us, that couldn't read the magic in the code we spoke with flesh and blood. We were ladies when our food arrived and guys when the check came.

You're a good butch, Raque-bebe. We can't lose any more good butches.

———

Sandy and I kept going back and forth.

It wasn't so much the fact that we started out as just another hot and heavy affair in the clichéd romantic simulacra of our making. A science fiction hot enough to melt an ice cap. My body will always remember its first Tucson summer—hiding out with Sandy for two days in one of Tucson's oldest neighborhoods, Barrio Anita, an address marked 666. Ours, a desire, fit for a beast.

Sandy phoned me later that evening when she was back at her home in Tucson. I had just returned home from seeing Lynn, Big Poppa's partner and now widow, as part of a large group of lesbians who had assembled in hopes of offering succor. We had gathered like the twelve disciples around Jeanne's lifeless body, which hadn't been moved from the bedroom yet, to offer a ceremonial circle, hands clasped to one another, to proffer her spirit with the lesbian pledge of love to who she was when she walked among us on earth. We were dyke Vikings sending her off with a pledge of devotion to her memory from that evening forward, as she moved to a Valhalla we knew to be peopled by other legends of lesbian activism. Losing Big Poppa was huge not just for me but for a whole generation of lesbians who wouldn't have language or culture if it weren't for her.

I thought about where Big Poppa's soul would reside now. Would she be with Yolanda Retter now, her rival and friend, an important librarian and archivist of Latina lesbian letters who called herself the gadfly of the body politic? I identified with Retter—another cantankerous butch in love with every femme in West Hollywood but too prudent and prideful to ever show a crack of vulnerability in her butch armor.

Nobody could afford to be a tender queer in those days.

When Yolanda died, Big Poppa eulogized her proudly, underscoring Yolanda's work with the National Lesbian Feminist Organization and her numerous other contributions to the ONE Archives at the University of Southern California and to the June Mazer Lesbian Archives in West Hollywood, as well her more personal and eccentric talents—Yolanda was a carpenter and an airplane mechanic who bought and sold rare books. Yolanda, using her gruff exterior to benefit a nascent lesbian community coming together in public for the first time in the 1973 West Coast Lesbian Conference, often directed security efforts as a chief monitor for community events. She was security coordinator for the people of color contingent for the first lesbian and gay March on Washington in 1979. She directed more security at the Los Angeles Dyke March and Sunset Junction, when the street festival was free and young Latinx families lived in Silver Lake. And Yolanda had, according to Big Poppa and Lynn, a knack for writing seventies-era button slogans that, in her own way, dissed and honored lesbian gender. "One sister's butch is another sister's femme," "You've just been served by a Lesbian," and "Marimacha, y qué?" A lesbian separatist through and through, Yolanda once stepped in the threshold of a lesbian gathering at a Chicana studies conference to ensure that no men—cis or trans—would be allowed to enter. Even Sandy could attest to that moment as she had been a young graduate student aghast at Yolanda's separatist tactics. Eager to inhabit the moniker "Yolanda the Terrible," she and Big Poppa once got into a fistfight over a femme that both had dated. I heard Yolanda swung first.

———

In bed again, staring up at the ceiling, phone in my hand. I had also broken the news to Sandy that David Bowie died on the same day as Big Poppa. We were both bewildered at the level of loss that day. The queerness of it all—two huge figures passing hours from one another, figures who bookended two important histories that buoyed the likes of Sandy and me, two queers at odds with the distinct worlds we were born into and who, with eight years between us, could still find common ground in our losses. She hadn't learned of Bowie's death because she was mid-flight from Texas back to Minneapolis, where she now lived. That move made our being together harder as she was now thousands of miles farther away from me than the mere five hundred between Los Angeles and Tucson. Just when I started to feel like we could bridge our differences, the physical gap between us widened.

Sandy coaxed me out. I wanted to belong to her. Give her my body, my secrets. Secrets that lived in well-hidden places, like the sky in Tucson that passed for the ocean when I was missing home. No one I was intimate with had ever thought to look up into the various constellations of shame that shadowed the life I was trying out for myself. Or to look down and see the mosaic pieces of my broken heart, a crushed ruby, hiding within the rubble of the gravel in the wash near her house. But she knew where to look, how to dig, pick up a shard and let the light shine right through it. And she was a good reader. A close reader. An interpreter of the ways in which my upbringing became the source of pain that brought me to poetry. And my poetry was what brought her to me.

I could have been an archival text, the way she studied my opaque marginalia with the intense monastic discipline I have admired in most scholars. She cracked my code. Sandy opened me so far wide I wasn't certain I was capable of closing myself back up again, a safety tactic I had somehow unlearned in her presence.

I read Eve Sedgwick's *A Dialogue on Love* when I found out it was Sandy's favorite, a book about how Sedgwick, a well-known queer theorist, begins a post-cancer therapy session but doesn't want to fall into providing prosaic responses that help explain away her depression, her anxiety, her codependences. I thought about the cancer regimen I had been spared and the cancer diagnoses Big Poppa had received over the years. The cancer that had finally stuck. I read the multitude of ways Sedgwick considers her therapist a love object and produces lyric poetry and haikus that obscure the wild constellation of neuroses she carries. Reading it was somehow sublime yet still pessimistic. I felt myself getting sick, the last chapter of the book placing me firmly into my own depression about Sandy.

It wasn't like we didn't have a shot at fully being together. Sure, we came from different worlds with distinct categorical markers, only to come together to create more distinct categorical markers about ourselves—I was raised by Mexican and Salvadoran immigrants in southeast Los Angeles; she was a Tejana red-diaper baby. Four generations earlier, the border crossed them, not the other way around. We were trying to reconstitute ourselves as a brown butch-femme couple while riding the wave of fixity that these identity categories proffered. We indulged in the romance assigned to two queers who longed to enjoy a gendered, butch-femme dynamic that emerged in surprising ways—the red in her fingernail polish, the dirt on my Redwings. It was a gender binary we kept alive in our private, intimate spheres. We were the *On Our Backs* centerfold that never happened. We had difficult childhoods, difficult parents, and we turned to various forms of nerdom to escape these soft prisons. We left our white partners for each other.

We were just like any other couple vying for happiness, despite the odds.

———

In the days and weeks after Big Poppa died at home, Lynn, newly widowed, along with any number of close friends and I would gather around the large wooden dining room table in revolving door visits to sift through photographs, articles, papers, and online tributes to the life of Jeanne Córdova. One image that easily caught my eye was a lesbian newspaper clipping of Big Poppa sitting in lotus position, a big smile on her face and a thin, bohemian, leather headband poking under her fallen pompadour.

What is this? I exclaimed like I had just panned for gold.

Oh, that. Lynn looked up and slowly smiled. *You know, Raq, this was at the start of Jeanne's desert period. She had just sold the business and went on a bit of a vision quest.*

Is this what Jeanne looked like when you two met?

I knew Jeanne and Lynn had met—as in all great love stories—at a lesbian support group in West Hollywood. Jeanne had just turned forty and was looking to start the next great chapter of an already storied life. I had heard many of these stories over the last few years as Big Poppa sat me down many times over diet cream sodas and menthol 100s and narrated the ways the lesbian and gay movement had both thrilled and exhausted her. Jeanne was the first at most everything where West Coast lesbian history is concerned. She helped cofound the city of West Hollywood, a bastion of protection for the nascent lesbian and gay community of Los Angeles. She was a delegate for a national gay and lesbian caucus at the 1980 Democratic National Convention, holding up a sign on the floor that said LESBIAN DEMOCRAT. But as she neared her fortieth year and saw all the ways the movement was moving right along, with new blood coming to tend the outgrowth from the seeds of change she had helped to plant in the early seventies, it made sense for her to interrogate her truer callings. New trails were what Big Poppa loved to blaze. I just didn't know that the desert had figured so prominently.

Jeanne loved the desert. When we first started courting, we would road-trip through the Southwest, camping here, really roughing it some nights in Jeanne's old Dodge pickup. Lynn's voice would quiver but she looked up like she was seeing the filmstrip of memory unfold over our heads. I poured her a glass of water from the pitcher on the table, careful not to sully any of the precious materials filled with important Big Poppa history.

And Jeanne really knew how to live. She'd say, "Lovey, how about we go to a hotel, get a hot shower, and then go antique shopping in Santa Fe?" The room erupted in awws and whoops at the gallantry that was Jeanne.

Jeanne loved the desert. We lived in Gamma Gulch for a few years before moving to Todos Santos. In fact, that's where she wants her ashes to be scattered.

———————

Gamma Gulch is a neighborhood—or what passes for one—in the exteriors of Yucca Valley, California. It is located next to the unincorporated community of Pioneertown in the Morongo Basin region of San Bernardino County's High Desert. The historical town was originally incorporated in 1946, cofounded by actors Russell Hayden and Dick Curtis, who had first "discovered" the parts just west of Yucca Valley while exploring on horseback a small swath of land nearby that Curtis had bought for filming Wild West flicks of the era. Other investor partners included Roy Rogers and Gene Autry, entertainers who brought their aw-shucks wholesome cowboy acts out west to Hollywood. The winding four-mile drive northwest to Pioneertown from Yucca Valley has been designated a California Scenic Drive. A place where people go as a means to escape their lives—where you go to fake your death, forget lovers, hide the body, or conquer whatever monkey's clutching to your back.

Today to hear of Yucca Valley and its more popular older sister, the town of Joshua Tree, is to hear of the government shutdown's impact on these small, sparsely populated high desert towns in response to the COVID-19 pandemic. People have come into the Joshua Tree National Park to steal or deface the largest of the yuccas, which grow only in the Mojave Desert. The Mojave yucca plant and the Joshua tree are the iconic fauna of the region, symbols of sun-soaked hardiness that proliferate every winter onto the IG timelines of our collective existence. They are sites of lesbian weddings for the witchy ilk who couldn't imagine finding the goddess in Palm Springs. It's where Gen X slackers came to pioneer Airbnb properties, ushering in an era of celebrity recreational occupation of these lands. Joshua trees are California icons, alongside the redwood, and are the kind of species anticipatorily grieved as the climate crisis continues to improvise its terror on the hottest pockets of the Southwest desert. The desert blooms of recent years have turned heads eastward to places like Anza-Borrego Desert State Park, whose 2018 super bloom was particularly stunning in a year that saw an uncharacteristically heavy rainy season. And, of course, for the last two decades the Coachella Valley Music festival has been forging relationships between millennials and Gen Z music lovers and aspirant hipsters and the desert. We didn't have Instagram in 2002, the year I saw Björk at Coachella. I was a twenty-five-year-old weirdo who stumbled into the desert oasis without any articulated hopes of capturing the most magical of magic hours. What was a selfie to a digital immigrant?

When Jeanne and Lynn lived in their part of the high desert, on the end of a bumpy dirt road on Gamma Gulch, Yucca Valley and Joshua Tree were in the midst of a desert renaissance. I imagine these two lovers clutching one another tenderly, their eyes adjusting to the dark purity of those desert night skies, teeming with stars. The kind made impossible in

Los Angeles. The early nineties were a golden era of sorts for music and art centered around Pappy and Harriet's, an old biker bar that catered to the motorcycle outlaw set of the seventies who roamed the highways surrounding the high desert. Serving some of the best barbecue outside of Texas, Pappy and Harriet's of the late eighties also served not only bikers but also the rough mix of locals, artists, Los Angeles nouveau riche, off-duty Marines from Twentynine Palms, cowboys and more hipsters barely surviving the winding five-mile stretch of death-wish roads that branch through the valley. On any given night you could chain-smoke under the Perseid meteor shower as you grooved to Victoria Williams or rocked out to Queens of the Stone Age while Ed Ruscha pontificated over kale salad just a few tables away. Or you could catch Jeanne in light denim shorts and a dusty Stetson Texas two-steppin' with her new girlfriend, Lynn, the cute ginger with the South African accent who had never dated a butch before. Lesbian lovebirds nesting in the desert, blending in with the other self-imposed exiled weirdos.

———

I had gotten laid off from a "good" arts administrator job in San Francisco when Sandy and I first started communicating. I was a "community arts curator," which sounded so meaningful, as if the praxis had somehow been more than just processing contracts and ordering catering and staving off the cultural takeover by our new tech-industry warlords. Within the organization middle managers battled to choose the artists and themes that would bring to fruition projects, happenings, small exhibitions, and public programs for a San Francisco demographic that was becoming more and more homogenous. It was bureaucratic violence meting out death by a thousand meetings that all should have been emails. Or in nonprofit parlance—organizational restructuring. Just as communities of color found themselves struggling to maintain their homes in a changing San Francisco culture, I suddenly found myself without a business card identity to buoy me.

My self-esteem was imperiled and so, of course, when Sandy made a series of butch-femme specific social media posts, I would post the occasional flirtatious comment. I thought I had some authoritative experience as someone who weirdly tethers herself to such a blatant label—a categorical marker to ensure my waning visibility.

All the back and forth on social media finally leveled up into direct message territory. I toyed with Sandy and sent her photos of me doing my best impressions of Cesar Rosas, lead guitarist for Los Lobos, since we both had pockmarked chubby cheeks, wore Wayfarers, and had an inexplicable cucumber coolness that read *puro suavecito*. She then purchased every chapbook I was selling through my tiny press. A few weeks of radio silence and then she wrote that my poetry had fucked her up. I read her message after returning from a weekend of camping in the East Bay with my white girlfriend and all of our queer white friends.

———

She said I seemed capable.

We were both in committed, monogamous relationships with white women who cared deeply about us. Yet it was precisely that relational configuration that enabled Sandy and me to offer each other shelter. There is something to be said about the comfort of recognition that comes from a lover or friend who looks like you, or at least looks at you like you are family, like there is familiarity in the ways you have both suffered. To find a lover who has been in the same position in the power structures that dictate our ontologies. We each saw the other's pain of misrecognition—such deep, howling pain about how our lives had escaped us. How we followed the trail of aspiration, stability, and still felt stuck.

After six weeks of messaging each other we agreed to meet in Los Angeles—I came from the Bay Area and she, the Southwest. It was one night that became a week. I was chasing a high. In between marathon lovemaking sessions that left me sweating, I gulped down copious amounts of French spring water like I had just conquered the Tour de France of fisting. And chasing the high got expensive. I racked up credit card debts paying for flights and weeklong Airbnb stays in my city and in hers. I was trying to prove to Sandy that I, a brown, nonprofit-class butch, would wine and dine her in the only way available to me.

———

Lynn had put out a call to the inner circle for help. I came over on a warm Southern California evening to relieve her of overnight care for Big Poppa. This was when the height of the cancer revealed itself in the roughest soul-shaking coughs that racked Big Poppa's thinning body for the rest of her days with us. Lynn was losing sleep on top of the mounting grief she was depositing in her emotional bank. And I was content to split my time catching a few winks on their leather couch in the living room, with an alarm set to wake me every two hours to give Big Poppa her pills.

It was midnight, which meant I hadn't even thought about sleeping, let alone felt the tug into slumber, but it was time to get Big Poppa's first round of medication from four separate snap-capped vials. A booming locomotive in the other room startled me to sit up suddenly.

Big Poppa? I whispered gently, hoping not to startle her, but Big Poppa was in deep slumber. *Big Poppa, it's time to take your pills.* Big Poppa stirred slowly, her eyelids fluttering open.

Can you help me sit up?

I pulled the blankets down slowly and felt the heat rise. I touched Big Poppa's bony shoulder and soft back and felt her long-sleeved pajama shirt soaked with sweat.

Which drawer do you keep your pajamas in?

I walked over to the tallboy dresser in the room and pulled out a new pajama top for Big Poppa. I turned on the lamp, sat on the edge of the bed, and gestured for Big Poppa to raise her arms over her head. I peeled off her nightshirt, her back hunched down, chest concave, and ran a dry washcloth to her underarms and shoulders. I quickly got her clean pajama top on to save her from catching cold, but also to preserve her butch dignity.

How's that? Better, yes?

I have to pee now.

Yep, I gotcha.

My body tensed up at the solicitation of a new intimacy, but I quickly let that pass through my body and assured Big Poppa that I wouldn't let her down. I took a deep breath as I bent at the knees and wrapped one arm around Big Poppa's lower back and put her arm around my shoulder. I slowly walked us through the night-lit hallway and turned on the lights in the bathroom. I lifted the toilet seat and helped Big Poppa pull her pajama pants down and then sat her on the toilet seat. She looked up at me and smiled meekly, though still mischievously, as if to say, *Can you believe this shit?*

———————

I got heart palpitations at the thought of my mother ever meeting Sandy. Sandy was not a girl, or at least not the kind of girl that would register on my mother's emotional radar. I was afraid that my mother would see me and say that I was the overgrown girl. Or boy. Or whatever awkwardly phrased term my mother would come up with to name my immature gender. I never heeded the signals of adulthood correctly— college, marriage, home ownership, children of my own. I saw my parents struggle with three of the four stages and it scared me into never aspiring toward a domesticity that could be reduced to a bumper sticker slapped crookedly on the back of my car.

Don't ever marry, my mom always says when we get to this part, when I come home after breakups with domestic partners. I guess she could sense that I wasn't cut out for that life. My mom married twice. It was what she had to suffer to survive her own growing up in the rural mountains, where El Salvador meets Honduras, and what she had to choose to make it out of there alive. I wanted to marry Sandy and I wanted that desire to find its bullseye. I had just returned my mother's rings but I wanted to ask for them back. I needed to make sure that desire fell on all the right reasons. Maybe I was too educated and too spoiled, and that meant never having to settle for marriage to strengthen my economic lot the way my mother had to do when she first got to this country. I also was too much my father's daughter and my mother knew that. My mother was my first riddle. She spoke a few words and fewer phrases, like codes to break down. She spoke them all like words cost money, so I was often left scratching my head trying to decipher whether I was cool or whether I was a fuck-up in her sad, hardened eyes. Marriage was never easy for her, and she modeled to me to find shelter in the world by relying only on myself.

Your father almost jumped off a bridge into the 710 [freeway] when his girlfriend left him. But that's what he got for giving her money I had saved up for our future. He's a coward and if it weren't for me . . .

Her voice trailed off but she left the hairs on the back of my neck standing straight out, the electricity softly shocking my body into the kind of submissive hold I had felt my whole life. She was prescribing me medicine or dictating my choices with a soft fist, a velvet glove. Did I not have what it takes to be in it for the long haul?

———

We watched the wedding video a few nights after Big Poppa had passed. Lynn, glassy-eyed, sat in the dark chocolate brown leather club chair that stood about fifteen feet from the large screen television in the sunken living room.

Wow, I marveled from my corner of the couch, watching Big Poppa in some King Arthurian-style velvet tunic stretch out both arms to Lynn, coming down an aisle in an unnamed outdoor setting. Women's music icon Holly Near had just sung their wedding march and taken her seat in the audience. Big Poppa is forty-seven in this video. Her hair is coiffed into a relaxed brush cut, soft sparkling eyes resting on her partner in crime, and her smile is easy, dazzling. *My god, this butch is charming,* I chirp to a roomful of swooning lesbians.

There were about six of us in Lynn's living room toggling back and forth between aww-ing and grieving, exhausted from taking turns to excuse ourselves from the room and go cry in private. In one of these flurries of exiting the room, bodies moved past me but I never tore my eyes from the screen. There was a close-up moment between Lynn and Big Poppa, a teasing twinkle in the butch's eyes and an utterance of supreme butch confidence that I hoped one day to spectacularly repeat myself: *It's not like you're marrying me for my money.*

I made my living that year in Huntington Park, traveling to present my work in a variety of cultural centers, museums, and universities. I was packing a suitcase while also unpacking my books, the evidence of some previous life I had spent developing my mind. There were so many books—novels and theory, proof that I wasn't always a nonprofiting paper pusher. Breaking a sweat and covered in cardboard box dust, I was trying to lay an order to my things while wearing thrifted basketball shorts and a threadbare white tee, the uniform of the neighborhood boys and young men I'd be passing on my way to various appointments with the world, a future I had to manifest otherwise I would go crazy. This was the bit of control I allowed myself after swallowing my pride and returning to my parents' home. The living room was a shallow sea of open-mouthed U-Haul boxes creating a maze between me and my smartphone when I heard the familiar bottle popping sound that indicated I had a new text message.

Can you talk?

I had to keep walking in the direction I wanted my life to take, as a teacher, a writer, a healer of sorts. A healer of self more than anything. I was done with what David Graeber calls bullshit jobs.

I was supposed to fly from Baltimore to Minneapolis to visit Sandy, but we fought and she uninvited me at the last minute. I ended up going back to Los Angeles, which had some divine timing to it. The weekend I had arranged to see Sandy in Minneapolis had become the same weekend that Lynn organized a mass lesbian outing to Yucca Valley to release Big Poppa's ashes into the stunning mammoth rock formations in Gamma Gulch. I thought I was going to miss the ceremony, but I ended up missing Sandy. Who was I kidding? Butch-femme relationships were a dying breed and here we were doing the dying, watching our previous relationships die, losing our patience for each other on top of watching our queer elders die. It was losing faith that got easy.

————

The twelve of us who were present on the first day of Big Poppa's death were also present for the day we released the last remnants of her earthly presence into the desert ethers. We packed ice chests filled with Diet Cokes into our cars and caravanned for nearly two hours from Los Angeles into the land of Joshua trees, their arms raised skyward as if heralding what we felt in our hearts. That our father was heading toward where she belonged. Freedom would soon be hers, arriving on the terms she fought valiantly for.

I plucked a hawk feather that I kept on my altar and stuck it in my shirt pocket that morning. Later I dipped it in the container and filled its tiny barbs and vanes with her ashes, the aerial ink imbued with the power of Jeanne Córdova. I raised my arms and let the feather go. I watched the ashes fly into the limitless blue above the boulder where I stood, the expanse of wild desert below. I swallowed the salt of my nasal drip, lit a menthol under my hat against the pounding wind, inhaled and raised my silver Diet Coke can to the only Big Poppa I would ever know.

Stuck in the Adobe

Earth is the rawest of raw materials.
—LUCY LIPPARD

2015 | I followed Sandy to the crumbling adobe shrine outside the El Minuto Café. The sun had set west beyond the railroad tracks and Interstate 10 yet El Tiradito was lit up by a chorus of flickering votives. A place for wayward Catholic pagans like me. And Sandy, a self-avowed atheist.

Tucson writer and friend Maya L. Kapoor says all of El Tiradito's stories "tend toward the lurid: gunfights, broken hearts, high speed tragedies. El Tiradito is a memorial; none of these stories have happy endings."[4]

Sandy took the paper folded in fourths and stuck it into the centuries-old adobe wall, alongside other petitions with their browned and frayed edges existing within the façade's well-worn grooves. This gesture gave me hope for continued connection, wondering how we would bridge our differences. It also made me question her atheism. Did she know what altars

---

4. Maya L. Kapoor, "The Castaways," *Territory,* http://themapisnot.com/issue
-iii-maya-l-kapoor/#canvas.

are for? Even if El Tiradito made a show of serving the hopeless, I wondered if Sandy could one day see me as being something beyond an undercover lover with holes in her sweater. How we could sustain ourselves, crumbling façade and all.

I knew I wasn't ready to be seen.

El Tiradito was right around the corner from her house in Barrio Viejo. She didn't live alone, but like anybody else in her predicament, she was very lonely. Sandy wasn't married but wore a Jewish grandmother's wedding ring on her left ring finger. It suited her Jupiter in Virgo to get married for practicality's sake. This wasn't a detraction per se but a mere complicated fact. Such details I have become versed in through my own creative pursuits—no judgment, just unreliable facts in learning the lores of other brown artistic types shaped by taboo, privilege, and unmoored libido. I was recently unmoored and struggling to find my footing against the tide—I was back, boomerang-style, living in the little house in front of my parents' house back in Huntington Park, a southeast Los Angeles neighborhood that went from white to brown in the mideighties. It was an old manufacturing Reagan Democrat bedroom community that gave way to immigrants fleeing the cold wars in their countries. I still licked at the wounds from having been laid off from my fancy arts institution job all while breaking up with my Bay Area girlfriend. I had the dream and then lost the dream just as Sandy came into the picture to moor my desires. The old picture tore itself up.

What was I getting myself into here? Were these just basic desires to comprehend, to finally grow into? Grow out of? Or was I destined to enact my own chaos that comes with the territory of being an artist?

———

2017 | Someone I knew posted a real estate listing of a house I was intimately familiar with, if only briefly. It was crass to see the amount the house was going for on Facebook. Is this what we do now? Peruse other peoples' selling power? Consider buying a rehabbed 1927 adobe home in one of the more expensive neighborhoods in Tucson's historic downtown barrios?

It was Sandy's house and two years after my first visit there. I started fantasizing about making the exorbitant purchase myself, melancholic in the Freudian sense, as a way to continue living with these ghosts. They needed more space. What could be better than an early twentieth century adobe?

I read the description in its realtor parlance and followed up with my own narration of each room. The bedroom with the hot pink accent wall. Its saturation come to life in my first weekend there.

I kept reading and I kept yearning. I reached the "truth wall."

———

The truth wall lives as a part of the room that exposes how the house is built. You see the unique materials that went into the skeleton—or how we know if the house has good bones. The truth wall reveals what we are surrounded by, showing its history in the sedimentary layers of adobe, bricks that live in the triangular crevice, deep in recess, high up where the wall touches the ceiling. An opening in a wall surface, the organic components within a wall, a century and its violences trapped behind spackle and stucco.

A truth wall might help increase the property's value. In the era where our desires for sustainable, climate-conscious living come inside a gold-level package of mercenary marriages—we marry up even when we want to slum—a truth wall or truth window often serves as a decor option demonstrative of our own interiors.

The truth wall silently nodded to the breakup that put it on the market.

———

Have you ever made adobe? Or wondered about the adoberos who made the large earth-sourced bricks that sit like ancient sacks of sugar on top of each other? Making adobe bricks is a process that requires repetitive motion of fingers, hands, wrists, arms, elbows, and shoulders as you're bent at both waist and knee. People have been making adobe since the tenth century. An ancient how-to manual by the early Sonoran Desert dwellers, the Hohokam, who the Tohono O'odham and Pima tribes descend from, and early constructors of adobe shelters might instruct you to dig a shallow trench in the ground using a well-pointed digging stick and to pile all excavated material inside of the trench. Then fill that trench with a three-to-one mix of mud and broken stone, or river pebbles, tamping thoroughly to fill all of the nooks and crannies. Dampen the mix only as necessary, using only enough water to soften the mud to a stiff moldable consistency. A penalty is incurred for anyone using more than the minimum amount of water required.

After the foundation has been allowed to set from one full moon to the next, place forms—three feet high, in six-foot lengths—around the perimeter of your chosen structure, inside and out, held almost two feet apart, weave twigs into a scaffold of mesquite poles in front of the slowly forming shelter, plaster with mud and allow it all to dry thoroughly for another full moon. Fill forms with mud that has been moistened only sufficiently to form a pliable mass, as used with the foundation, puddling thoroughly but using water sparingly. Tamp with bare hands until form has been solidly filled. For an example of ancient adobe handiwork, see the Casa Grande National Ruins in Southern Arizona, constructed by the prehistoric Salado tribe.

———————

Everything that made this mud—the water, the soil, the straw, occasional blood—must be strong enough to hold a house together.

You need a lot to make a stable foundation, to build walls capable of holding difficult truths.

———————

The truth is often too much to traffic in, so it makes sense to put it behind a wall. You make a crack, clean the edges, and place a piece of clear glass in front so you know that it's there. You turn the truth into an object and say it's in the room with you, even when you come up with daily modes of obfuscation. Versatile is a truth able to keep you cool in the summer heat and warm every winter.

———————

It had been two years since the last time I saw these adobe bricks in triangular formation, tucked under the slant of the roof of your house. An early twentieth century adobe home, a transformed Sonoran remixed in place on a one-way street in Barrio Viejo. It was Halloween the weekend we spent together, but we didn't dress up. I passed out candy while you graded papers. You became agitated when I asked why you and she never did a couples' costume. I said you two would have been a perfect Trotsky and Kahlo. You gulped down your Manhattan just after setting a pair of martini glasses in front of me. "Let's go inside," you said, changing the subject, your tone coming up for air sweetened by the whiskey.

———

2017 | I had spent the hottest part of the Arizona summer in Patagonia near Nogales. The border scorches—even above a set of mountain ranges that means the air is ten to twelve degrees cooler. It means a high of 96 degrees instead of the 108 back in Tucson. It means I can return some oxygen back to my coastal California-raised brain and body. I was not unaccustomed to hibernating in the middle of June.

I was in a unique place, one of the most diverse in all of the United States, for Patagonia is distinguished by six ecosystems encountering one another—the Sonoran Desert meeting the bottoms of the Rocky Mountains and the Sierra Madre butting up against the Chihuahuan Desert leaning into the Neotropics flirting with the high desert's grassy wonderlands.

I had booked it out of Tucson to beat the heat and avoid heartbreak's niggling little ghosts. Restoring habitats using sustainable ecological methods was a good place to start. Methods that required younger, stronger bodies to put their hands into the soil. The environmental study that hooked me into gifting my labor.

That meant having to muster whatever elbow grease still existed inside of me, parsing it out from the usual reserves of lactic acid that typically resided in the vessels between muscle and bone. Getting up early meant shooting cold brew down my throat and chomping on organic, sugar-free beef jerky to ensure some protein could prop up my body with nutrients that would undoubtedly sweat themselves out. I trimmed mesquite trees growing on a steep incline, dug up irrigation systems overlooking red eroded buttes, and weeded amaranth out of squash crops while bent at the knee. *Man, this is the food of my ancestors,* I thought bitterly, pulling at the greens.

By the end of day one my body ached, my spirit burned. I had to do my part to forget my heartache by breaking my body open.

This was essentially an internship at forty, and the skeptical Jiminy Cricket lumpen proletariat in me restlessly ruminated about the unequal division of labor between the owners and the contracted labor there to tend to their land. I am just one generation out from a broken Mexican economy that we left to come north, seeking better opportunities. Well, not *we*, but *he*—my dad. He settled in Los Angeles in the early seventies after following various commodities—potatoes in Wisconsin, plastics in Texas, strawberries in California. He, embittered by the time I came along. I grew up weary of his moods as well as any exploitation of my labor. Protecting myself against both, a daily task.

But I wanted this, so the apprentice I became. It was an art I wanted to learn. I wasn't selling my labor—I was learning a skill.

I wanted to do my part in creating a relational map—to make, see, and share the worlds we could actually belong to if we could sustain the intimacy. Talk and then listen; dig up the remnants of the earth we shared to then pat it back down tighter. Walk the wounded back to themselves and encounter a little bit of healing for myself along the way. That was the hardest part—to see *and* accept what might be readily offered to me without my anger or suspicion obstructing something so needful. I wanted to be and stay in the room with the pain of others and trigger the wherewithal to mark my own way back through the underworld of myself.

But something changed on that third day of borderlands restoration. My curiosity piqued when we were asked to make adobe bricks.

————

I arrived at the Deep Dirt Farm to a crowd of volunteers around Kate Tirion, the proprietor, who was giving everyone instructions on how to clean an outdoor compost toilet. Tirion was a spry and strong seventy-something who, after a cancer scare in her sixties, pivoted into the healing properties of permaculture. It made me recall my own cancer scare back when I was living in the Bay Area. For two weeks, I didn't know if the enlarged lymph nodes under my arms had bad cysts or the plain, not-bad kind. For two weeks, I wondered how I let my life lose its color, its volume, all while possibly incubating cancer near my breasts. Tirion chirped me out of my reverie and into her strong Welsh accent. How fortuitous it was that we had arrived to learn such an important cornerstone of sustainability culture as she vigorously (and audibly) churned the bowl with her composting rake. The gut-rocking stench coming out of that outhouse made me question such fortuity.

I was happy to move away from the outhouse, especially because painful fibroids were in the midst of turning my uterus inside out—bio-matter surely connected to my irregular cystic lymph nodes. I would have to come inside this compost toilet to deal with golf-ball-sized blood clots shooting out of me every couple of hours, though I did manage to comfort myself with four ibuprofens and the thought of blood being put back into the earth. It had a very Anzaldúan quality— helping the border's wound heal with the runoff of my body's internal properties. It was a way I could refuse to let my body's messy condition take its emotional toll.

There were other messes to be made. We moved toward the mud pit where we would be sourcing materials to make three hundred adobe bricks that morning. None of us would be going home with clean clothes; I knew that from the previous two workdays with the restoration crew. I braced myself to soon be covered in mud, straw, and whatever species called those things home.

———

2015 | *Is this Frida blue?* I asked, gesturing to the walls of her house as we made our way to the front door. The entrance of her front patio was trellised with Mexican birds of paradise, like we were suddenly transported to Coyoácan. I looked both ways to make sure Diego wasn't around.

I walked into the foyer and saw *Mujer Angel,* the famous photograph of a woman with her back to the camera walking toward the Sonoran Desert with a boombox. Sandy was writing about Graciela Iturbide's photographic oeuvre as it pertains to border ontology. The photograph stunned me, shielding my silence from any scrutiny. I looked around the entrance hall and saw the truth wall behind a huge painting of a sacred heart—the classic, bulging red aortic rendering, not unlike what you might see in Mexican lotería cards, against a sunburst yellow background. Above it hung a garland of red chili pepper lights. The strange wall dividing the rooms felt anachronistic, with its salient texture a muddy glow against the shiny, gunmetal-gray concrete floors, and the earth-toned living room furnished in Copenhagen Imports behind it.

I didn't want to know its story just yet. Of how brown art lived there, possibly even thrived. Near the adobe, on the adobe, beside the adobe. The spoils of hard work by the artists that lit up the foyer is not an art for art's sake. Yet the bricks that laid atop one another sealed a different history within a house that was built in the old barrio in 1927.

———

1927 was an important year for Tucson's architectural progress, that progress second only to Charles Lindy Lindbergh's "Spirit of St. Louis" skating down Tucson's Davis-Monthan Air Force dirt-ground tarmac in a cloud of dust, finally stopping for him to exit the small airplane. The pilot would later be known for the violent death of his kidnapped child and his isolationist position in leading the America First Committee, an organization against joining the allies to help Great Britain in World War II. A would-be Nazi sympathizer, Lindy was guided to a Sonoran Desert succulent sculpture, "Spirit," made of the region's renowned ocotillo and other cactuses (designed and fabricated by local florist Hal Burns), where he posed with and greeted officials. His visit to the southwestern city four months after his historic trans-Atlantic flight was part of a 22,000-mile, forty-eight-state tour sponsored by the Guggenheim Foundation to promote air commerce. It was a hot day that autumn afternoon, and Tucson was a city on the precipice of growth.

By the late thirties, Tucson was poised to meet the twentieth century once and for all. According to Tucson historian Lydia R. Otero, the city's public square, known locally as *la calle,* had landed in the crosshairs of zoning officials interested in making Tucson not just a bigger city but a better one. The emergence of the 1966 Pueblo Center Redevelopment Project, the state's first major urban renewal project, included "plans to build several government buildings, a modern retail complex, and as its showpiece, a new performance arena and community conference facility, the Tucson Community Center," known today as the Convention Center. As a result, Barrio Viejo arrived as a seventies-era post-development neighborhood simulacra following the renewal initiative in which a long stretch of adobe homes and storefronts was contoured from the remnants of three early twentieth-century Tucson neighborhoods—Barrio Libre, Barrio El Hoyo, and Barrio Membrillo—creating a residential myth that appreciates in value. Or, as Otero suggests, Barrio Viejo came to be through a "destruction of a large Mexican American community through urban renewal in the late sixties fueled by the idealization of modernity, a local economy increasingly dependent on tourism, and the evolution of federal housing policies."

Tucson's urban core found itself typified into more territorial-period adobe buildings than were found in any other part of Tucson, and its intact Mexican-style urban streetscapes were unique in an Arizona always striving toward leaner and cheaper housing booms. These urban neighborhoods reflected the spatial vernacular of the Sonoran, transformed Sonoran, and transitional architectural styles that, over time and the mountains that stood in Manifest Destiny's way, came southwest with eastern tastes and imaginaries. While some carriers of those tastes came west to escape such conventions, others brought them along with the intention of civilizing the old pueblo, one barrio at a time, once and for all.

———

We arrived back at Barrio Viejo. Sandy beamed at me, lying on her couch, drinking her wine, and reading the poetry books I'd found in corners of her living room. *I* was maybe too comfortable. We were on that cosmic planar velocity, our compatibility revealing itself to us at breakneck speed. We finally settled into her couch and watched a movie. She shifted so much she jostled me out of my little spoon spot in the concave of her body. I felt her body heat up, a quickened pulse practically thumping into my spine.

Are you feeling anxious?

Before she could answer the inevitable, I felt something gushing out of me. I rushed into the bathroom next to the truth wall. It was the first time I knew something was not right with my body.

———

2017 | *Who wants to stomp in the pit?* Tirion called out to the crowd of mostly local high school students awkwardly shifting back and forth at the task she had laid before them. I was grateful for these young people emanating the skepticism I was hoping to obscure. Stomping would help soften the soil, water, and straw for easier brick molding, but I wondered if I could push myself through these new thresholds. I was surprised by the collaborators who went for it. They walked past me, unaware of the numerous ways the thought of sullying myself paralyzed me. Being in their presence took me back to my own internship days, as the only brown kid in a hallway of predominantly European art and conservation professionals, up on the hill where the Getty Center was, back in Brentwood, California. The young people here, though, were local to the area—the children of ranchers who rolled up each morning in late-model, big-wheeled American trucks along-side the children whose parents worked on their ranches.

Five of the young high-school-aged women offered to get into the pit with Tirion's friend Michael, a local chef and con-noisseur of seeds, which he kept offering to people as a seed mix, a multitude of tiny colors inside a clear sandwich baggie. Michael was breaking down soil from the embankment, half circling the mud pit with a large shovel; the mud reached him at mid-calf.

I was overwhelmed by the severity of contact with the wet earth. It was the rawest sensorium I had encountered, and I longed to surrender to it. I thought of the mess outside meet-ing the mess inside my body and retreated.

———

2015 | I was giving myself away. I had never bled so much on the first day. Provisions could not contain me. My body started feeling unfamiliar to me. Was this aging? Or was my body try-ing to stake a claim on a lover who'd never fully be mine?

I left a trail of bloody tears from the bedroom all the way to the bright white subway-tiled floor in the large bathroom. *This is so much blood.* We had to change the sheets twice in less than thirty-six hours. I even soaked through the mattress. I won-dered how she might explain that after I had gone.

———

2017 | The next assignment required the wheelbarrows. And Kate Tirion wanted to know who was going to help fill them and carry the muddy booty back and forth between the pit and the molding area. I longed for a role of such important utility, so I volunteered, hoping some activity would calm the painful itching from an attack of fire ants, their anthills so common in the desert.

Plunging my hands into the mud pit felt like dropping a cannonball into the deepest part of a swimming pool. It was exhilarating. Had I found the amniotic sac I had been desperate to return to, hoping to be spat back out into the right side of history? I felt my hand in the softest part of the earth. I didn't want to let go.

The softest parts are often the heaviest. I had to recall my core muscles to get that mud into the wheelbarrow *and then* not drop it all over the ground. I took my first batch to where the brickmakers waited and watched them with hands alone scoop their batches into the molds, their backs bent, sleeves rolled up as they fashioned big birthday-cake-sized mud bricks with careful precision.

———

After Patagonia I was off to Marfa, Texas. I had been invited to read at the community's inaugural poetry festival and was glad to be venturing into the West Texas landscape by myself by car. That August marked a year alone in Tucson and suddenly the desert felt like it could belong to me, no strings attached. Like I, too, could project a semiotics of self-discovery and reinvention as some kind of lulling counterpoint to the settler colonial fantasy that lived in the marrow of such fictions. I staked my dream onto the desert.

Finally passing Van Horn, I detected the Milky Way above inching itself closer to the roof of my car, its purple galaxy swirling me into reverie. *Can't get used to losin' you. . . .* I reached for the sole beer I had been saving in my cooler and

pulled the tab open. I took a long sip and let the hoppy good-
ness swish around inside my mouth. There was no one on the
road except me.

I knew of Marfa's lore—a weird, high art vacation destination
that pulled coastal elites into its western promise of freedom
and untapped possibility. I also knew that the railroad tracks
divided the brown community from the white. It would be
interesting to be there while my friend, the artist rafa esparza,
was in the middle of a summer residency. He had received a
prestigious commission from Ballroom Marfa—the people
responsible for commissioning that famous fake Prada store on
Highway 90 just outside of Valentine, Texas.[5]

Welcome to Marfa. I had no signal whatsoever on my phone
and hoped I could find rafa's summer house. I stopped in a
Dairy Queen parking lot and used the restaurant's wi-fi to pull
up the map pin that rafa had dropped in his last text to me.
I was glad I could recall reading a map without the GPS lady
intoning orders to me. Thankful for all those years of reading
Thomas Guides in the back seat of my father's 1982 Mercury
Zephyr. I managed to find the spacious bungalow in tasteful wood grain and metal-colored earth tones with a mud-
splattered, white pickup truck parked out front.

Dang, rafis. Rafa came out of the house wearing a cream-
colored shawl and ushered me inside. It was so good to see
him, happy and thriving in this strange place offering him

---

5. *Prada Marfa* is a permanently installed sculpture by artists Elmgreen and
Dragset, situated 1.4 miles (2.3 kilometers) northwest of Valentine, Texas,
just off U.S. Highway 90.

unabashed support for his art. New York–level support. He was hitting the big time. We stayed up until two in the morning recounting recent heartbreaks and hair-raising encounters with law enforcement in the borderlands while drinking fine mezcal from a bottle that looked straight out of the Tudors.

By the time I woke up the next morning, rafa had left for his "studio," an open field next to the hipster hotel where he had built a muddy bank next to a pile of straw. He had been making hundreds of adobe bricks all summer. His show opened at the end of the month, so the clock was ticking. I had only gone three days without bleeding and, of course, it started again that morning. That marked six months straight of bleeding. The doctor I saw back in Tucson put my gold-star lesbian womb on birth control, and the adjustment was proving difficult. I made sure I had my provisions and left the house to find my way to the mud pit. It would be a collision of messes, but I was ready.

Seeing Marfa by day activated all the complicated nostalgia meridians in my body. There were street signs that rung of old-timey Americana and the water tower that boasted MARFA on its belly. But it was still West Texas; its history of denigrating treatment of Mexicans spilled into the quotidian, and that reality never escaped me. Still, I felt a star-crossed romance for this doubly crossed place, as my friend the Los Angeles writer Rubén Martínez denotes aptly—Marfa is a place that boasts:

> railroad tracks upon which trains clacked through a couple
> of times a day, meaning you could hear bona fide train
> whistles—enchanting for any city boy or girl. The tracks,
> of course, also meant that there were another side of them,
> where the "Mexicans" lived; that's what they called them-
> selves, and what everyone else called them, too, in spite of the

fact that many of them were second- or third- or fourth-generation on this side of the border, speaking Spanglish, English with a Mexican accent and Spanish with a gringo accent. On that other side of the tracks sat the adobe ruin of the town's old segregated school.

I soon met up with rafa's team: Rubén aka Fresca, the queer baby femme Chicanx multimedia artist from El Paso, who was on mud duty, mixing water into a fresh swath of soil and straw. And Sandro Canovas from Mexico City, the hetero-intellectual whose life's work examined the Mexican history of adobe architecture, was carting mud back and forth with the wheelbarrow. Fresca urged me to wear a weightlifting belt for protection, so I donned one and helped shovel mud into the wheelbarrow, trying to keep up with my stronger collaborators. But they took pity on me after seeing me nearly drop the wheelbarrow full of mud one too many times and handed me a pair of knee pads. They said I would be better off washing the brick molds and making bricks with rafa. I happily obliged, though I knew one task wouldn't be any easier than the other.

In Los Angeles, rafa had made his name as the artist who invited anyone and everyone to come make adobe bricks with him. The bricks became his frames, often laid out as the floor of any given gallery or museum. The adobe transformed these traditional sites of artistic presentation. Down with white walls, down with white cubes. Forgoing the decolonizing rhetoric and opting for indigenizing these art practices, brown artists could present in a visual vernacular that resonated with their immigrant and Native origins. An homage to his father, who built his first familial house in Durango, Mexico, out of adobe with his bare hands. These bricks, for rafa, call on that ancestral

knowledge as a way to center immigrant labor practices in the
u.s., bringing into the sight line those who have been marginalized by the avant-garde and the art market. An homage to
those protected by the mud of madre tierra.

It was finally my turn to help him make bricks, a practice
that had always scared me off with its demand of intense physical exertion. But I was there, ready to sweat and ache, to find a
way to stave off the spasms of want that haunted all of my days
that year. I dug my hand in the wet soil. It wasn't the first time.
Each time always came with a jolt, a feel-good oxytocin-like
high that surprised me again and again. It was here this whole
time, beneath my feet. It was one thing to walk barefoot on a
concrete-less earth, to feel blades of grass between my toes.
But plunging my fingers, hands, and wrists into the terrestrial
mix felt ecstatic.

———

I ran into Sandy at the coffee shop in downtown Tucson two
days after returning home from Marfa. But isn't that how we
run into our exes these days? In the coffee shop, checking their
social media presences that confirm their material absences
in our lives? It had been a year since we had last seen each
other. She jumped into a new relationship a month after ours
ended. I was still single but about to hit-and-run several relationships. She and I differed when it came to the classic lesbian
conundrum of U-Haul dating.

I sat down at her table, hubris or desperation fueling the
coming soliloquy. Sandy didn't say much besides *I don't know.*
I kept asking the same question in a dozen ways: *How are you?*
I looked at her with soft eyes. *If there was ever another chance
to do this again I would.* I let my voice trail off while my hands

white-knuckled the Topo Chico bottle that had become slippery with sweat despite my grip. She finally looked away.

―――――――

I left the coffee shop in a victorious stupor. *She hadn't said "no,"* I thought to myself. I went home with a renewed sense of desire for what could be, yet knew the odds weren't in my favor. I was a meme that made fun of Pisces, but I didn't care.

I don't know which was more self-induced—the sabotage or the delusion. But I chalked up my magical thinking to the ancestral seizures that occur on hikes or other communes with the nature Tucson offered. Seizures in the capturing sense— where I feel oceanic toward the desert's beauty, a beauty permeated by the slow yet painful realization of colonization. It's a pain that punctuates every encounter since then and the histories I'll never be able to undo for those who came before me. Seizures that compel me to wonder at the hummingbird sitting still in the mesquite or the moth landing in my lazy pompadour as I wander and wait for the sun to set over Gates Pass in the Western edges of Tucson's city limits. Seizures as in maybe my ancestors were telling me not to give up on her, filling my head with the language of retrieval. Get her back. Is this why we make art? To chase or attract? Lover or muse, angel or devil, ancestral memory or unhealthy obsession—my duende sought her out.

Everywhere I looked Sandy's laughter and melancholy remained imprinted over these difficult terrains from Tucson to Marfa. Even walking Donald Judd's concrete structures found me cursing the prison of desire closing in on me. I was walking the labyrinth in perpetuity, lockstep with her, as one absence gave way to several others.

————

These tropes might register in that familiar way that threatens their originality. But I had never felt this way before and the arrival to a new language takes time.

————

When we first started communicating, I would jokingly suggest to Sandy that she leave the hacienda and join the revolution.

————

I brought my altar to the shrine of the sinner. A petition for my lost lover to make her way back to me. And the only place that could house my humble-yet-unreasonable request was El Tiradito. A place built on the burial site of one Juan Olivares, an eighteen-year-old worker who began an illicit love affair with the doña of the hacienda he worked for in a changing Tucson after the Gadsden Purchase of 1854. Some stories cite the object of Olivares's affections as his mother-in-law, but a story of classed desire seems more plausible considering the impenetrable caste system of the day. Olivares was shot and his body dumped in a nearby ditch where neighbors buried him on the spot. A few months later, people began to notice miracles taking place, inspiring them to build a chapel in honor of Olivares, the one who was cast out.

A yellow candle, a couple of cigarettes, some yellow flowers stuffed into the same Topo Chico bottle I had clutched earlier that day, and a sign taped to a couple of old drum sticks that read: *Regresa A Mi.*

SECTION II

DIFFICULT TERRAINS

Do Migrants Dream of Blue Barrels?

2017 | I live in Tucson. People tell me they love the images they see on my various social media feeds of the mysterious, moon-scape desert that surrounds the city. Many of the friends, acquaintances, and strangers who follow me on social media live along both coasts, so of course it gives me great plea-sure to ignite their awe for the uncontainable beauty of the Sonoran Desert, even if from afar. For me, being in this desert on any given morning or early evening means giving over to the expansive possibilities of the landscape. It has offered new perspectives when I'm stuck on a writing project—stepping out into any number of trails and parks and contemplating the day's ebbs and flows. Whether it's the way the light moves across the shallow valleys of Gates Pass before sunset or the way the temperature surprisingly drops ten degrees when your trail takes you into the shadowy parts sitting below Pima Canyon, the infinity of surprise that lives here is hard to deny.

But as 115–120 degrees becomes the new normal for Southern Arizona, indicating a climate change that may not be reversible in years to come, there is another thing one can-not deny—any slight carelessness on your part and the desert will kill you. That fact made itself clear on a ride-along outing with Guillermo and Stephen, two volunteers for the regional organization Humane Borders/Fronteras Compasivas. As soon as I climbed into their water replenishment truck, I was told that if we broke down in Arivaca—an hour and fifteen minutes south of Tucson—we would be exposed to the same conditions as the Latinx migrants we were trying to help. I stared dead-eyed behind my Ray-Bans at Guillermo—we would never be exposed to the same conditions as migrants making this trek.

I shook off any doubt that we would not be okay. All of us engaging in humanitarian work should have it seared into our minds that we are the lucky ones. After all, we were traveling with more than a hundred gallons of water into the harshest topographies of the Southwest. At worst, in my mind's wandering to worry, we would be sweaty and uncomfortable while changing the imaginary flat tire—but we wouldn't die.

I made contact with the privilege I carried into different parts of the valley that surrounded the infamous border town Arivaca, though I wasn't sure I could ever make peace with it. In this part of the country, whatever you did or whoever you were—if you were somebody's anchor baby; a pedantic gadfly; a broke bourgeois bohemian who cared about justice and human rights and had heated conversations about immigration policy with family members during the holidays; if you still wrote diversity statements for scholarship applications, or ate nopal fries and drank aged whiskey cocktails with the liberal, latte-sipping NPR listeners in downtown Tucson, where the adobe facades were restored to look like the old pueblo—you came and faced these incongruent truths, maxing out credit cards to do the thing you did in the name of justice. If there was anything to do with your privilege, it was to risk it. And it would never be enough.

————

Humane Borders maintains a system of water stations in the Sonoran Desert on routes used by migrants making the perilous journey north mostly by foot. Each station has its own name: Green Valley (Pecan Orchard), Elephant Head, Rocky Road, K-9, Cemetery Hill, Soberanes, Mauricio Farah, and Martinez Well.

Getting into the truck at Green Valley, we were promptly driven to the first water station, situated behind a pecan orchard. The orchard looked momentarily out of place and time with its trees lined up tightly, towering above a few acres covered by bright green grass, an indication of the obscene amounts of water the plants must have consumed on a daily basis. But I was thankful nonetheless for its place in the landscape and hoped it would offer some shady respite to the men, women, and children who made the orchard a part of their journey.

As soon as we got to the water station, I quietly gasped at the sight of concrete blocks, a quartet of two-by-four wood planks, and a fifty-five-gallon blue plastic barrel sitting stoutly but bravely above the desiccated arroyo. These objects in any other home improvement configuration might not have inspired such deference, but for me it was like seeing Stonehenge in real life—or rather, seeing these water stations gave me the same feeling I had when visiting Stonehenge as a high school sophomore. These artificial structures made eternal the belief of vibrant life lying beyond the little world I was trying to escape.

These monuments remind me of what we are willing to confront in order to sever ourselves from fear. We are all trying to leave something behind, emerge from the rubble, and go toward something better, and there shouldn't be any guilt or fault in that desire.

But, of course, that desire is deadly for many.

What does it mean to exist in structural conditions that erode those desires for peace and happiness? How did the wealth gap determine one's ability to survive economic and natural catastrophes? It shouldn't be this hard to move toward safety. I'm a beneficiary of those who have made similarly arduous journeys to safety. I have been spared the experience of crossing the desert to abandon the threat of physical and social death from my birthplace of origin. And relying on my imagination has revealed an ontological poverty. Standing at the crux where foreign agents make the draconian state out of these unceded Tohono O'odham lands makes that knowing possible.

These water stations are myth come to life, a border fable peopled with heroes and rogues, monsters and saints in search of the magical elixir. "No More Deaths" is a declaration one might encounter in a fairy tale. Only in the fabulist space might death be no more. A decade earlier, I'd hear of No More Deaths from rafa back home in Southern California who, a few years before I met him, had come back from a desert trek with our mutual friend Alan to do humanitarian work at a camp managed by No More Deaths.

Fear makes it hard to be here and the cortisol makes it feel like my innards are short-circuiting. My body is here to meet the risk; that is what it's about, right? I will be the distraction so that somebody less privileged can make their escape. I will make space in the back seat where I sit, absorbing the bumpy impact over difficult terrain. I sit and look out the window again, my gaze falling on the peaks of the Baboquivari Range. There are so many things I do not want—an arrest, jail time, a felony. My mind rushes through the crashing waves of this dangerous futurity and I am not brave enough. I think of Scott Warren, a volunteer member of No More Deaths arrested for helping migrants to a safe house near Ajo. Warren, a lecturer at the Arizona State University School of Geographical Sciences and Urban Planning was arrested in January 2018 and charged with two counts of harboring and one count of conspiracy, which are felonies. Warren faced a retrial in November 2019 and could have received a prison sentence of up to ten years if not for his acquittal.

———

Do migrants dream of healing elixirs photosynthesized with the cancerous UV rays of the sun? Do they spot the plastic gallon bottles situated at the base of the ocotillos that obscure vultures and other carrion birds, perched in wait?

———

2018 | I go to Arivaca for lunch with A one late winter day. A is a good friend of mine who works with No More Deaths, another gender weirdo who's been this close to receiving felony charges for illegal transport of immigrants. Through A, I've met other queers who I might have spotted at punk shows in Oakland or Los Angeles or standing in line at the co-op in Brooklyn. Many an anarchist punk has made their way to Tucson to work for No More Deaths—so much so that No More Deaths feels like some kind of queer rite of passage into

Tucson's radical communities, where any given Friday night sees a wild mesh-and-Day-Glo, Bay Area-style dance party fundraiser for undocumented queer and trans people, sometimes specifically to raise bail funds for queer organizers caught in the crosshairs of draconian border policy. I love A's tales of hooking up with fellow aid workers who come through for the summers only. Sex and No More Deaths together have a very plutonian quality—the intensity of the work that takes place in the desert inspires a most unique eros.

That day the shore of the Arivaca Lake was still quiet when A and I stopped at La Gitana Cantina for a quick cold beer. Scott Warren hadn't yet been arrested, but No More Deaths was the necessary revolution, much to the chagrin of Arizona's conservatives. What was the alternative to letting people die in the desert?

A picks me up in their dusty, decade-old Nissan truck. We stop at the co-op in Tucson for olives, anchovies, crackers, and kombucha before jumping onto the highway and then winding through the mountain roads that spit us out three miles from the border itself. The town is Wild-West tiny with a colorful general store and a saloon jumping into my sight line. It's too early for a round at La Gitana Cantina, but that doesn't stop the parking lot from being packed at eleven in the morning. A parks in front of the Arivaca Humanitarian Aid office to introduce me to the lovely aid worker, whose name shall remain anonymous, who welcomes me in and speaks to me in a familiar Spanish, narrating a day in the life of the town that feels absurd after seeing fleets of border patrol trucks and wondering who might be eyeballing A. I buy a T-shirt and take a few photos of the "people-helping-people, border zone" murals that portray a Disneyesque pastoral landscape with desert wildlife hiding behind traffic cones and stop signs.

———————

Living in the borderlands, you count among your friends and neighbors those who want things to be different here. We use our time to stay aware, to be in service. We live here to embody the lesson that everyone should be entitled to improve upon the conditions of their life. That often means leaving behind a pressure cooker combination of corrupt governments, violence, and barren lands. Those lessons arrive differently for us. We are people connected to immigrants and migrants in deep and complex matrices—as their children, their lovers, their friends, their bosses, their customers, their neighbors, or if we are lucky, their students. Some of us will never know that direct experience of moving across harrowing terrain. We will never know the hard choices made to begin those journeys. Some of us work in networks of care that rely on a rapid response strategy that provides the most vulnerable travelers with funds, warm clothes, or a place to stay after leaving the detention centers that dot the southern Arizona landscape.

And sometimes, if you're like Francisco "Paco" Cantú, your connection is a complicated relational dyad that will haunt the rest of your days. Cantú spent four years in the Border Patrol and distilled those experiences of tracking and arresting border crossers—and the moral injury those actions produced—in his memoir, *The Line Becomes a River*.[6] His book was released to much fanfare, ingratiating him with the liberal media and putting him in the crosshairs of border activists, who angrily challenged him on several platforms for capitalizing on migrants' deaths through his art-making. While some of this critique is echoed in Tucson, the reality of our lived days

———————

6. Francisco Cantú, *The Line Becomes a River* (Riverhead, 2018).

is that to see a border cop with some *toque de Mexicanidad* is a quotidian event. And it's time to reckon with why Mexican Americans, the children and grandchildren of Mexican immigrants, decide to don olive-green pants and green-and-gold-patched white shirts to police southern Mexican and Central American migrants making the journey north. Why do these inhabitants of southern Arizona divorce themselves from the recently arrived? What is gained by enacting these distances? What are the proximities they make way for? I struggle with these questions as a way to understand my own kin. I ask more questions.

Why did my Salvadoran immigrant brother, fourteen years my senior, join the Marines after barely graduating high school? Why did he become a Los Angeles sheriff's deputy? How did we happen to share the same uterus at different times? It's time to unmake the quotidian, to learn from those who have permanently damaged themselves by carrying out our draconian and inhumane policies from the inside out. To a more privileged subject like me, this quotidian conundrum brings a sense of doom to all my other like-minded efforts: voting, calling my senators and representatives, tweeting my outrage, unleashing tiresome tirades to trolls whose worlds seem to get bigger while mine diminishes with activists and scholars dying early deaths.

I often get asked if I know Francisco Cantú—but he's just Paco to me. Paco the well-read, soft-spoken king of the nerds who brings up Cormac and Anzaldúa in the same breath and will only discuss mezcal distillation processes if you specifically ask him about it. I get asked if I support the border patrol because I like his tweets on occasion. *This is Tucson,* I say. *You can't change the past.* In a red state known for denying Mexican American high school students a chance to learn about their histories by banning ethnic studies curricula, it means a lot when anyone is willing to step up for the disenfranchised. You can't change the past, and it's hard to be the ideal advocate in Tucson, where authorities very literally made it impossible for young people to even learn about the region's past. Living with the past is the hardest burden day in, day out, seeing the ways tensions improve between Mexican American and Indigenous communities or don't. I don't want to build false dichotomies, pitting one group's past against another's as a way to defend certain histories. Harnessing those energies for a solidarity where we center the migrant's plight feels more important to me.

————

2016 | My dad sheepishly admits that the reason he hasn't gone back to the gym in his neighborhood is because he accidentally hit the gas instead of the brake and totaled his minivan by slamming it into a light post in the gym parking lot. It must have been bad, I said. He laughs. At seventy-five he doesn't often give me the backstory to his mistakes and any story is usually filled with omissions too painful to remember. I think of the story he shared with me over a crab dinner that he splurged on in Fisherman's Wharf after riding the Greyhound all night to San Francisco, where I was living at the time. In the late sixties he was arrested for working without papers in San Francisco and was placed in custody for a couple of days on a fishing boat in Alameda, California, cleaning the deck until agents found him a bus going to El Paso. This was a time when being detained meant nothing more than a ride to Ciudad Júarez or Tijuana while Mexicanos on both sides of the line listened to the band Los Tigres del Norte, of San

Jose, California, sing earnestly about contraband and betrayal in a transnational drug deal between lovers gone wrong. That golden age where you got back on that hill, grassy and lush, and tried it again until you got it right. And he did. My dad got that part right.

————

I started thinking about the ways in which the untraceable is made evident, or how the migrants' journey has been represented to me throughout my life as both a young reader and writer—the Los Angeles-born, eighties child of parents from El Salvador and Mexico—and as the adult child, living in the here and now. In prose, we have writer Rubén Martínez of Los Angeles who, in his nonfiction book *Crossing Over: A Mexican Family on the Migrant Trail,* describes riding with the Chavez brothers, Indigenous members of the Purépecha tribe from the town of Cherán, Michoacán, in search of a better life. But how is a life made better if it means working in the rural Arkansas poultry industry, where people will call ICE on you at a moment's notice? We also have Reyna Grande, rendering firsthand, without mincing words, the very particular experience of crossing over. People come north because the alternative is death. These writers portray others or themselves as desperate to reunite with family in the North, all in various pursuits of better economic stability.

For me as a reader, these voices have meant finding the language to illustrate the ways migratory traumas continue to haunt families both constituted and torn apart by inhumane border policies. But my own parents' migration took place in the late sixties and early seventies—they were essentially crossing an imaginary wall with nary an agent in sight to police such boundaries. Or they simply overstayed their visas, as my mother did. She was a nurse in San Salvador who came to the U.S. fleeing a violent husband. She stayed in Los Angeles in the early seventies, dare I say in the heyday of border crossing, innocence on par with episodes of *The Brady Bunch*? Or the golden age of border law breaking, captured in that scene from *Born in East L.A.* where Cheech Marin's character Lupe interrupts his own privilege as a Los Angeles-born-and-bred Chicano to find himself caught in the Kafkaesque bureaucratic nightmare of unlawful deportation. The climax of the film happens when Lupe, atop one of the many hills scattered through the borderscape of Tijuana and San Diego, summons the migrant masses with the elegance of an orchestra conductor to run down the hill and overwhelm two slack-jawed border patrol agents who have underestimated the ethnic disempowered other, per the usual.

———

2017 | Back in the truck, I felt myself dolefully assign the landscape its benevolence, something to help muster the belief that what we were doing would make the slightest impact. It was Sunday. Of course, we all had the same thought that morning—would we encounter anyone in need of our help?

———

Do migrants dream of blue barrels in the middle of the emptied ocean floor? Hiding in the brush in this harsh wilderness, dying under the weight of the sun?

———

In the distance, I stopped and listened closely: an intrepid purple flag waved in the hot summer wind, its color dulled by the daily solar pounding of summer.

After surveying the water station for cleanliness, potability, visibility, and instances of possible tampering, we moved on to the next one in Arivaca proper, Elephant Head. But before heading out of the pecan orchard, Stephen asked Guillermo to stop the truck on the periphery, where he spotted empty water bottles and a spectrum of detritus left by migrants past. Plastic bottles that were empty but still intact signaled recent passage. However, there were also old, discarded backpacks that, like the people who had carried them, were now empty and succumbing to the harsh conditions of the merciless desert. These bits of human evidence made the area seem anachronistic—to travel by foot in a time saturated with every imaginable technology. This was our refugee crisis.

It was not hard to sense that specter of migrant death nearby or in my third eye. Everything in that mise-en-scène blinked like a neon sign—migrants who came through the shade of the pecan trees more likely than not found their downfall in the washes around Arivaca, eleven miles from the border itself.

2017 | The border and the imprint of migrants' deaths left in its hinterlands animate most experiences I have in the surrounding nature. There's no natural encounter—passing by a saguaro or seeing a mountain range silhouette at sunset—that doesn't have the uncanny attached to it. The beauty of the desert never exists in a vacuum for me, like art for art's sake. This sentiment is approximated for me in the artwork of my friend Karlito Miller Espinosa who, like me, left a coastal metropole for Tucson in 2016. An artist known for his exquisitely executed murals—from New York to Kiev—he started working in conceptual registers that allowed for a more direct critique on the cultural zeitgeist in which he found himself. His three-dimensional installation pieces in Tucson are centered on cement bricks made from sand and debris collected from sites around the southern Arizona borderlands where migrant bodies have been found. *Untitled (Corridor), 2018* is a work that organizes the bedlam produced by U.S. immigration policy on the border space of Arizona and Mexico into a compact, narrow corridor. Fueled by a desire to ensure a futurity, most migrants are Indigenous men and young families leaving the dead ends delivered by their native countries, where industries were sold off to the highest bidders and allowed free rein in a post-NAFTA world. Just as Mexican artists Teresa Margolles and rafa esparza comment on how violence intervenes in the daily lives of the most vulnerable in both Mexican and U.S. society, Karlito, too, offers a much-needed elegy for the migrant who comes north to labor. He brings land to art. And while the bricks themselves innovate on a page out of minimalism, to experience them against the antiseptic walls and floor of a gallery space allows for the Sonoran Desert to leave its locale and trouble the viewer who is otherwise comfortably distanced from the deadly terrains. For me, Karlito's work troubles me through the reminder of the debt I owe to the migrants, the uncomfortable intimacies that contour the histories between us, and the circumstances that reinforce the tensions.

———

I am a passenger watching the scenery of the borderlands beyond the brink of madness. We are all—at least the lot of us in the vehicle making this trip—a mere tithe to the desert to spare the living crossing through it. Every day could be marked by a colorful crucifix.

Over the next nine hours, covering nothing more than the stretch of six miles at three miles per hour, we were all mad. Or obsessed. It is this affective drive that has compelled volunteers like Guillermo and Stephen to make the same trip every two to three weeks for the last two years. No one should go through this. Everyone should run thumb and forefingers into the bullet holes of signs around the water barrels. Everyone should come close to being trampled by the cattle roaming freely. No one should risk this. Everyone should notice the wake of buzzards flying too close for comfort. No one should be separated from their families. These imperatives shouldn't fall on the luck of the draw.

―――――

2017 | When we arrived at Elephant Head, I noticed something that wasn't on the first blue container: *La Virgen de Guadalupe.* Or, rather, a glossy sticker with her likeness.

All my twelve years' worth of nostalgic Catholic school hackles go up at the sight of the feminine deity who made her debut on a hill in Tepeyac, Mexico. An apparition that, today, only an Indigenous man re-christened Juan Diego under similarly violent conditions could witness. As chronicled in the mid-seventeenth century tract *Nican Mopohua,* Juan Diego Cuauhtlatoatzin was an Indigenous man born in fifteenth century Mexico, when it was still Tenochtitlan. A subject of the Aztec empire, Juan Diego was caught in the crosshairs of colonization. He was an early adopter of Catholicism, opting for baptism over complete subjugation. In 2002, Juan Diego was canonized as the holy witness to the apparition of the Virgin

Mary, who appeared to him on the hill of Tepeyac in 1531 and exhorted him to build a shrine to her there. Did praying to the Virgin with Indigenous features make it easier to believe? This, of course, is relevant because Tepeyac is the site of a recently destroyed shrine to Coatlicue, the mother deity in the Aztec polytheistic tradition. In 1531, just as autumn transitioned into winter, Juan Diego returned from a fourth encounter with the Virgin and opened his tunic, spilling luscious red roses onto the floor. This gesture also revealed the imprint of the Virgin Mary's image on the cloth of his humble vestment. Roses would have been impossible to grow in the cold spell during that season.

Stephen noticed me noticing her and said it's a way to show migrants that the water station is there to help. Stephen, a civil rights attorney for the ACLU, reminds me of the aging, white Central American solidarity folks back in Los Angeles. He reminds me of the kind of men who would teach me about the parts of the Salvadoran Civil War that my mother would omit. I nodded, affirming his assumption and hoping that non-Catholic migrants would be able to decipher the tank as a site of relief. But behind my sunglasses and smile I bit my lip and pinched the muffin top peeking over my belt to keep the flood of emotions at bay. When will the colonial encounter finally pay its debt to the migrant, the descendant of those who, under duress, chose the one god of Catholicism over the many gods and divinities of Aztec/Toltec/Mayan cosmological spirituality for the variety of supplications that emerge in a life?

I pull the soft red bandana from my back pocket and rub it over tear-streaked cheeks and sweaty brow.

———

As the morning progressed and the sun's rays intensified, I felt the perspiration pool in and around my body's various concaves and then disappear. The desert was taking its rightful tax of moisture from me, collecting its debt like it does every day. We snacked on sweet baby peppers and threw the ends out the window. Guillermo said that it would be a few hours tops before the desert consumed our biodegradable trash. We went on like this for hours, our bodies flirting with being untraceable all while traversing Arivaca's veins and arteries.

Time seemed to be marked by how close or far we were to a curious mountain peak known as Baboquivari, a sacred place for the Tohono O'odham nation. The creator, I'itoi, resides in a cave at the base. Baboquivari represents a genesis of sorts. Or where to return for many. Throughout our ride-along, Guillermo would stop for all of us to take in the scenery, snap photos, and stretch our legs. It felt like Baboquivari was looking out for us as we did our best to look out for others. Back in the car, rolling at our near glacial pace, Guillermo—an old punk like me who lived for a decade in a northeast Los Angeles neighborhood (like me, again) but now lives in Tucson (yep, me, too)—regaled us with a story about his dying grandmother. He had traveled from California one spring break years ago so that he and his cousins could gather to camp and pray for their Yaqui grandmother's health. They passed a joint around as they hiked up the mountain to Baboquivari's peak. Being young men on the precipice of adulthood, they silently competed with one another—who could walk faster? Who could carry the most gear? Who could keep up?

I was not going to let those guys know I had a flu, Guillermo said, carefully guiding our vehicle over sharp, rocky terrain, *but I was dragging behind them when I felt something watching me. It was a mountain lion, and I turned around so quickly I scared it away.* The rest of us in the car sighed in relief collectively. But Guillermo wasn't going to let us off the hook. *Did you know,* he begins, *that a mountain lion loves to eat a fresh kill? He'll sneak up behind you, take a swipe at the base of your neck, bite down on your cerebellum, and paralyze you.*

Wait. *Wait. Are you basically watching yourself get eaten alive?* I ask, looking out toward Baboquivari, hoping for the hundredth time that hour that we don't break down.

———

I touch the amulet in my pocket, a piece of black kyanite, moon-charged with protecting energies. That is my metaphysical response to the circumstances currently beyond my control. I want to turn my energetic GPS on so that my ancestors can find me, protect me somehow. Our guides are continually asked what happens if we encounter migrants on these trips: Stephen says simply that they are to be given food, first aid, and water.

No one mentions felony.

No one mentions the way that your right to vote or to secure gainful employment becomes jeopardized with the mere provision of water, food, and medical aid to a migrant found wandering in one of the deadliest deserts in North America. We were wanderers with maps and GPS, Havarti cheese, and herb crackers. We traveled with more than a hundred gallons of water and a full tank of gas. We traveled with the privilege of knowing our way back home.

Behind the Barrier: Resisting the Border Wall Prototypes as Land Art

2018 | The easiest way to visit the border wall prototypes begins in one of the day lots in Otay Mesa, the little strip of soil sandwiched between the Brown Field Municipal Airport in San Diego and Tijuana's Aeropuerto Internacional Abelardo L. Rodriguez.

There is so much I want to do to cut the intensity of this visit. I want to drive further into Tijuana and eat, my favorite way of quelling any storm that rumbles, or walk on the broken concrete until I find the next sensory distraction. But there's no time for that. As Michelle—my traveling companion—and I walk the few short blocks to the Otay Mesa port of entry, I am reminded that the thrashed earth on the other side of the rusted, corrugated fence is also America, one that comes with an accent mark over its middle syllable. Gripping my fairly new and little-used u.s. passport, I reflect on the fact that, for me, this short journey is meant to be a smooth one, uncomplicated. Yet it's not—these days, it can't be. Maybe I should have scrubbed my social media of any political positions before venturing south.

This is what traveling to Tijuana has been like recently—tinged with a fear of becoming more other, more suspect, than I already am. More queer. More brown. More susceptible to being noticed. When I was a kid, my parents would take us to Tijuana to see the dentist, to fill prescriptions more cheaply than we could in our southeast Los Angeles neighborhood. Nowadays I have friends in Los Angeles who opt to bring their dogs to the Tijuana vets for cheaper care.

As the crossing comes into view, I feel myself growing closer to what my parents left behind and further than ever from those who live in true precarities of mobility—lifelong friends whose poetry I love, who've slammed back tragos with me over heartbreak and hard-won victories, and who wait for news of green cards and amnesty. I am suspended in the haze of that spectrum where danger is always in theory. But anything could happen and laws change like goalposts, adjusting to fit the victor's needs in a fixed game.

Both Michelle and I are tightly scheduled and highly organized on this visit to the prototypes before heading to our mutual friend's wedding in San Diego later that day. The time for the trip shouldn't—can't—last more than three hours. It's not even ten in the morning, which makes me feel doubly responsible. I am looking forward to toasting the aging punks of my youth later that afternoon as a vexed palate and soul cleanser.

Michelle and I pass a famous, ten-foot-tall sculpture of a Mexican man and woman, colorfully clothed in serapes and flowers. There is a velocity to the captured movement, a dance trapped by time—*Fiesta Jarabe* by Luis Jiménez. The sculpture seems jovial and out of place—at least to anyone who's made anxious by borders. We cross the pedestrian bridge into customs. Michelle and I walk across the pedestrian bridge and get in the customs line. I photograph everything I see, even the sign that says no photographs allowed. This gets me into trouble: the security guard barks at me to put my phone away. I blush and offer a meek *perdón*. *Te dije,* Michelle says, shooting me a teasing look. I glance down at the passport peeking out of the chest pocket of my denim jacket. I am a citizen playing dumb, I think. A Los Angeles-born Mexican with a Salvadoran mother spending a quiet Saturday morning witnessing the material convergence of art, monument, and xenophobia.

Finally, it's my turn to greet the customs official, an olive-skinned young woman with vermillion-hued highlights heightened against the olive drab of her uniform. She asks my intentions in México. I am short and the counter stops at my shoulders. I am honest with her. I want to see the border wall prototypes nearby. She looks up suddenly from stamping my passport and looks me in the eye—really looks me in the eye and the rest of my face. My twinkling Muppet eyes and big dumb smile disarm her, as does the light brown suede Tejana cowboy hat on my head and acid wash denim jacket on my body. I am a brown neon sign: aimless aging homosexual hipster with attachment issues. She practically suppresses an eyeroll as she gives me back my passport.

According to the coordinates on my phone, the prototypes are not very far away, less than five minutes up Boulevard de las Bellas Artes, followed by a loop around the maquila zone tucked in the hills behind this section of Tijuana's main drag. I don't have an international phone plan, but I figure we'll stay close enough to the border that it won't make a difference. On the other side of the bridge, the taxi drivers are a spectrum of khaki pants and white oxfords, leaning against crumbling concrete facades, drinking coffee and putting out their last cigarettes before the mass of tourists come stumbling through the port of entry ready to make a mess of their México. Michelle and I find an older driver named Manuel who knows exactly where we want to go. He's intrigued by the two of us: we are older than the average co-ed, plus Michelle's Spanish is very much reflective of her upbringing in nearby Chula Vista, whereas mine is Salvi singsong.

We tell him we're educators. Manuel suddenly turns fatherly and begins to narrate President Trump's recent springtime visit to the border. Manuel tells us many Tijuanenses were aflutter in anticipation that Trump would step foot in their city. *Trump came all this way and didn't have the guts to face México.* But then I remember that we came all this way just to look back into the U.S.

———

In an August 2016 campaign stop in Phoenix, Arizona, Donald Trump criticized Hillary Clinton for not centering American citizens in her concern that migrant families seeking asylum would be separated at the border. He promised that the United States would be "fair, just, and compassionate to all," but that the greatest compassion would be reserved for American citizens. That speech is worth revisiting, especially since it conjured a future we in the Southwest have started calling "the present," where thousands of migrant parents have been systemically separated from their children. Trump used the promise of a wall, the denial of these migrant families, as a means to get elected. For four years, the Border Wall came to stand in for Trump himself, a metonym for his presidency. Chants of *build that wall* echo in reverse to "Mr. Gorbachev, tear down this wall," the famous Berlin

Wall speech delivered by Ronald Reagan in West Berlin the summer I turned eleven. In a campaign stop in Anaheim, California, Trump, newly invigorated by an endorsement from the u.s. Border Patrol, spurred a crowd to chant *Build That Wall!*

The border wall prototypes made their public debut in October 2017, with six contractors vying for the job. u.s. Customs and Border Protection (CBP) evaluated the designs in five categories: breaching, scaling, constructability, engineering design, and aesthetics.[7] ("The north side of the barrier should be pleasing in color and texture to be consistent with the surrounding area.")

Aesthetics.

CBP hired engineers from Johns Hopkins University to develop a test to determine which design was "most beautiful." As a report from the Government Accountability Office states flatly, "CBP identified three prototypes that ranked highest in terms of attractiveness and participants' perception of effectiveness."[8]

There is more of this inadvertent arts writing in an ekphrastic Associated Press article quoting Border Patrol spokesman Terron Francisco: "the models, which cost the government up to $500,000 each, were spaced 30 feet (9.1 meters) apart. Slopes, thickness and curves vary. One has two shades of blue with white trim. The others are gray, tan or brown—in sync

---

7. Jack Balderrama Morley, "But Are They Pretty? Government Grades Border Wall Prototypes on Effectiveness and Aesthetics," *The Architect's Newspaper,* https://www.archpaper.com/2018/08/border-wall-prototypes-tests.

8. United States Government Accountability Office, "Southwest Border Security: CBP Is Evaluating Designs and Locations for Border Barriers but Is Proceeding Without Key Information," July 2018, https://www.gao.gov/assets/gao-18-614.pdf.

with the desert."[9] Some fanfare about two of the potential contractors presenting prototypes made of materials other than concrete. This doesn't feel "in sync with the desert."

———

In January 2018, a Swiss artist named Christoph Büchel took advantage of a residency in Los Angeles at a well-known and even better-resourced gallery to guide participant-spectators from the Museum of Contemporary Art in San Diego into Tijuana. The tours were a way for Büchel to spread the gospel of his provocation—that the prototypes be considered seriously as land art; that Donald Trump be considered a conceptual artist. People flipped out, which was of course the point, and he was accused of aestheticizing state violence toward immigrants coming north, amplifying the currency in which Büchel traffics. Artists outside the country had a conceptual playground in the u.s.—we had an unstable tyrant at the helm of the First World who ate Big Macs in front of Fox News, drank Coca-Colas and yearned to push the red button that would destroy our enemies. We didn't know that we would be living the stuff that would drive the art market into its own frenzy.

What Büchel did recalled the tradition of what many East Coast and European artists have done with and to the western regions of the u.s. Declaring the desert landscape a "nothingness," ready to be swept into grander aesthetic visions, is not a new practice. Maybe Büchel recognized something familiar in

9. Associated Press, "Prototypes for Trump's Wall, Including Israeli Model, Take Shape on Border," *Times of Israel,* October 20, 2017, https://www.timesof israel.com/prototypes-for-trumps-wall-including-israeli-model-take-shape -on-border.

the prototypes. He saw the artistic history that informed the way each prototype sat situated between two countries.

The following month, in February 2018, I read art critic Carolina Miranda's article in the *L.A. Times* recounting her ride in the Mercedes-Benz van that took her—along with other curious spectators, journalists, and one art historian—to witness Büchel's "intervention."[10] *Donald Trump is a conceptual artist.* I'm not surprised to learn that the gallery Hauser & Wirth (annual revenues: $225 million) would champion this work.[11]

Büchel—whose previous provocation involved building a mosque inside an unconsecrated Catholic church at the 2015 Venice Biennale—is barely legible as the author of this border spectacle, an artistic sleight of hand hidden behind a gallery website that makes bare mention of his name.[12] An art world so cozy with itself. I'm losing half the day trying to find the artist's signature. Am I a part of this meaning-making now? I think about making the most of lost time and plan a trip to the western borderlands.

When I write to Miranda asking for more information about the prototypes, she replies quickly, sending me the coordinates.

---

10. Carolina A. Miranda, "Is It Inspired or Irresponsible to Call Donald Trump's Border Wall Prototypes 'Art'?" *Los Angeles Times,* February 8, 2018, https://www.latimes.com/entertainment/arts/miranda/la-et-cam-christoph-buchel-border-wall-prototype-20180208-story.html.

11. "Top Ten Art Dealers," *Forbes,* May 3, 2012, https://www.forbes.com/pictures/mgg45egdg/4-iwan-wirth-42/?sh=3f34e7450074.

12. Randy Kennedy, "Police Shut Down Mosque Installation at Venice Biennale," *New York Times,* May 22, 2015, https://www.nytimes.com/2015/05/23/arts/design/police-shut-down-mosque-installation-at-venice-biennale.html.

———

For the Department of Homeland Security, the Border Patrol's operational requirements for the border wall prototypes considered such things as "aesthetics, how penetrable they are, how resistant they are to tampering and then scaling or anti-climb features."

Aesthetics, as I have understood them in my several decades of working in the arts, are the ways we observe and understand information through the senses. If we're lucky, we'll find beauty. If we're smart, we'll find ways to convince others of said beauty and sell them a membership to an institution. I felt a pang of sickness at the thought of the sensory overload these structures would cause for those encountering them coming from the south to the north on foot, after scavenging for water and foraging for whatever edible thing the desert offered, surviving rape and murder with breathing bodies but living in the perpetuity of social death.

Six vendors constructed the eight prototypes, with one company building two of the eight examples. These companies are Caddell Construction Company of Montgomery, Alabama; KWR Construction of Sierra Vista, Arizona; ELTA North America Inc. of Annapolis Junction, Maryland; W. G. Yates & Sons Construction Company of Philadelphia, Mississippi; Fisher Sand & Gravel Company of Tempe, Arizona; and Texas Sterling Construction Company of Houston, Texas. ELTA, a large Israeli defense contractor owned by state-run Israel Aerospace Industries, which opened a new office in Maryland in 2012, paid $406,319 for its contract. ELTA strayed from the desert color palettes of the other prototypes and instead offered six light blue squares with white trim on the bottom third, topped by dark blue beams and metal plates. KWR

Construction Inc. earned $486,411 for its contract. The company, located just twenty miles north of the u.s.–Mexico border, presented its prototype as gray metal columns topped with a large metal surface. KWR is a small company founded by one Arthur W. Rivas and located in Sierra Vista, Arizona. Their website mentions Davis-Monthan and Luke Air Force Bases and Interior departments among its clientele.

———

When the prototypes were finished and installed just below the Otay County Open Space Preserve, located in the Otay Valley Regional Park just four miles north of the international border, it wasn't hard to see them through a contemporary artistic lens. The regional park extends about eleven miles inland from the southeastern edge of the salt ponds at the mouth of the river, through the Otay River Valley, to the land surrounding both Lower and Upper Otay Lakes. It also wasn't hard to imagine Fox News having a field day imagining "the illegals" ruining their pastoral possibility projected onto this last bastion of open space. Across the valley on the u.s. side of the border stood fences marking off access to the prototypes that looked like huge sculptures. But it wasn't just concrete that held court in the horizon line that the prototypes, side by side, created together. Multiple materials were making meaning upon an exhausted palimpsest.

———

For the uninitiated, land art, a shortened catchphrase for "landscape art," is any artwork that utilizes natural elements in harmonious congruence with an outdoor location. The process is meant to work within the physical context of the environment, which means the work tends to settle itself among the forces that will alter or destroy it. *Spiral Jetty,* Robert Smithson's iconic work, uses 6,650 tons of basalt, boulders, mud, and salt crystals mined from the area around Rozel Point on Utah's Great Salt Lake to form a massive spiral that winds 450 meters out from the lake shore. The ramp that leads to the sculpture is eroding, both by the natural progression of a salt lake basin under climate change's duress, as well as by the work's exposure to people.

I made my own pilgrimage to *Spiral Jetty* in May 2018, surprised by the level of fanfare present on a Wednesday. The shrieks of aggrieved preschoolers filled the otherwise calm environment, where just the right bit of sun pouring through the billowy white clouds shows up as red on the lake's salty water surface.

For fifty years, the land art movement has stirred up many an art student to abandon paintbrushes and take up concrete blocks against the art establishment, to stand with these coastal mavericks articulating new, large-scale expressive modalities. In an art school context, stanning for land art has always been a line in the sand, one that states that the performance and sculptures standing largely outside of market forces hold faithful to the tenets of artistic freedom. When I worked in an arts institution in San Francisco, colleagues would plan land art road trips, where one could roam freely (with four-dollar-a-gallon gas) through the Southwest in search of Smithson's ghost. And, more important, one could behold these earthworks as they were meant to be experienced—in the vast space of western landscapes unencumbered by the trappings of modernity. I tend to be drawn to fanaticism and fan culture, so I bought in, too.

Art, the land artists contended, could be a liberatory project, one that upends the gallery and institutional system, and is perhaps best exemplified in a series of 1,500-foot long, 50-foot deep, and 30-foot wide trenches in the earthy landscapes of Overton, Nevada. In 1969, Michael Heizer's *Double Negative* displaced 240,000 tons of rock, mostly rhyolite and sandstone, to compel spectators to consider how art informs our relationship to the land.

Heizer was born in Berkeley in 1944 to a prominent anthropologist father. This legacy apparently influenced the younger Heizer to explore Native histories and cultures, seizing on the concept that nothing exists in that part of the Nevada desert *except* for an invitation to tear into the earth—never mind that the territory was inhabited by Shoshone, Washoe, and Ute tribes before and after the Treaty of Guadalupe-Hidalgo.

Situating the border wall prototypes in this history, I think, conjures the anarchy of consequences put forth by history then and policy now. Half a century since *Spiral Jetty* was constructed, maybe it's time to consider how the architects of land art have reproduced a version of Manifest Destiny—one that stretches from the corners of lower Manhattan to the deserts of the Southwest. The wall—in whichever flavor of prototype you imagine it—marks the boundary, the extreme limit, a beyond brutalist demarcation of that tradition. The mere thought of the prototypes allows for the wall's aestheticized form to emerge not just in the material of the border but in the collective imaginary.

———

While I never made it to *Double Negative,* I did find my way to the other side of the Great Salt Lake in the Great Desert Basin side of Utah. I drove up from Salt Lake City and the highway took me momentarily through Wendover, Nevada, where I stopped at a familiar site and ordered a bean burrito from Tacos El Brasero, which serves an array of red and green salsas and mouthwatering escabeche from a makeshift counter in a converted horse trailer on the edge of town. *El brasero* as an object is typically a brick stove you might find in a Mexican kitchen. It's a heater, a controlled fire pit. But in my mind it's also the homonym for *bracero,* a laborer. I smiled at the young Indigenous woman, said *gracias,* and commented on the dark clouds overhead. I headed back to my 4Runner and looked out onto the last big town for the next forty-five miles. I drove back again into Wendover, Utah, the skies sending me into a Freudian sense of the oceanic. The road was empty except for one gas station where I wondered if I could pee in peace while

I pumped a few gallons for the just-in-case. I crossed into the looser graveled roads and passed the TL Ranch. I kept driving until I saw the dramatically contemporary orange arrows pointing me toward Nancy Holt's Sun Tunnels. I passed a crossroads that caught my attention because they were the kind of crossroads I sought for any necessary communions with Eleggua, the mischievous Yoruba deity of the crossroads, the trickster child messenger I have been in contact with for much of my adult life. The drive to Sun Tunnels was as good a time as any to offer my gratitude for safe passage. I had a few trinkets and candies in the glove compartment and made a mental note to stop on the way back.

On that day Uranus stationed into a new sign of Taurus. Would I feel any shift in energy as I moved through these new terrestrial pathways? Something new was giving way. What was it? I wandered along the astrology podcast that had been scoring my thoughts into another great, wide-open space. The astrologer said that Uranus ruled sudden changes. She suggested that the Tower tarot card relates to the kind of change Uranus might be responsible for, and I thought back to all my tarot readings in the Bay Area, asking a brilliant trans writer what it means when the Tower card showed up over and over again. Taurus is the antithesis of change, but it rules money, systems of value, investments, beauty, rich foods, and sex. But the podcast astrologer I was listening to on the drive also asked us to focus on the terrestrial nature of the symbol's animal figure—the bull—and our current climate crisis. The fact that it takes 1,800 gallons of water to produce a pound of beef. That this astrological shift into a new energy might ask us to consider new plant-based foods. That there would be food shortages. That the earth is demanding that humans adopt a new mode of relating to it or bear the consequences.

The astrologer's was the only voice I heard as I turned on the last stretch. I saw what looked like lead pipes in a cross configuration in the distance and felt myself wince in warm anticipation. I parked at a respectful distance and walked toward the tunnels at high noon. I knew Nancy Holt owned the terrain I walked on, but the fact of my solitude in the there-and-then eclipsed that fact. It felt like the land belonged to itself and these immense tunnel-like structures were an anachronistic homage that channeled the sky's light into intention. I sat in each tunnel, noticing each cylinder's configuration of smaller holes representing the stars of four constellations—Draco, Perseus, Columba, and Capricorn. Ptolemy's greatest hits in four directions.

I walked back and forth and diagonally into each tunnel. I was a needle sewing a button. It was nearing high noon but the sun was softened by the cool winds, the hue of blue so languid and lush it felt like the sky was draping itself over the desert basin. I lit a glass candle I had brought from Tucson—an *abre caminos* (road opener)—for my time in each cylinder as an exercise in stillness. The flame struggled on the wick and my lighter overheated. Am I trying too hard?

In her essay "Tunnel Visions: Nancy Holt's Art in the Public Eye," Lucy Lippard writes that Holt's masterpiece is neither "monument [nor] memorial" to the memory of Holt's husband, Robert Smithson, who died in a helicopter crash on July 20, 1973, near Amarillo, Texas. Yet, the site itself, Lippard writes "offered an extraordinarily relevant way in which to mourn, to contemplate, and to build a future at the same time."

The noontime sun meant that everywhere I walked would be marked by the long shadow ahead of my feet. I was alone with too many of my selves. I conjured the many conch shells I had heard over the course of my young adulthood, how its muted horn was released into the ether in each of the four directions. I thought of the times I have made fun of these cosmological expressions of faith and energetic exchanges structured by the Chicano studies classes my generation took back in the learning halls of greater, lesser, and East Los Angeles. I think of the poor ways I was taught to construct relationships to the ancestral past that determined these lands. To rely on the phenomenology of resistance and Chicano movement-making as a root for a spiritual practice. I remember the Aztec danzantes on Alcatraz during one recent San Francisco Thanksgiving, ushering in the sunrise ceremony with dance and drum. How those dancers crafted costumes in the image of a warring Mexica peoples. And how I moved my body to the east, west, north, and south right along with them. Mexico made it all the way to where I stood until 1848, itself a powerful machination in the systematic enslavement and removal of Indigenous people from the territories I had been driving on and through for the last week. Maybe my philosophy was cringe-inducing—I was an urban Aztec in prayer, light-skinned mestizx long distanced from any experience of Indigeneity that saddled my Salvadoran grandparents who grew up in a time in the early twentieth century that made it dangerous to be a Poor Indigenous Person. Ysaura and Catalino became common-law married, birthed twelve babies, and raised the nine that survived in El Saucé, a valley hamlet in the northeastern mountainous region, a reasonably safe distance from the western departments of El Salvador that were at the center during La Matanza at the start of the new year, 1932. They hid themselves in the iconographies of the savior, the country's namesake and reason for the many instances of Indigenous bloodshed. The first because they were savages. And the second, communists.

It felt ancient and I was exhausted of being interpellated by images of Catholic belief—the dead girls and the waifish monks, pagan murderers, and tenacious scribes—saturating available mystical possibilities. I found the Zapatistas the year I graduated high school; their aggrieved dispatches against the many ways the North American Free Trade Agreement would upend their culture were the anarchist cookbook whose recipes fed my desire for a different world.

I stepped out of the tunnels and into the directions they faced like portals and raised my palms in salutation.

———

2018 | Manuel drives us quickly and then slowly through the Nido de las Aguilas neighborhood, the two gas stations per block indicative of a neighborhood mapped by its proximity to the border, roads pockmarked by huge eighteen-wheelers carrying their loads to the clamor of consumers poised and ready for product. It is early on a Saturday, so we don't see the young girls queuing in and out of the maquilas, huge hangar-like buildings surrounded by fences topped with terrifyingly sharp barbed wire coils. The dirt road is parched but along the fences there are gutters of oily colorful prisms glowing in the putrid runoff. In the other direction, a rusted corrugated fence looks puny in comparison with the scale suggested by the prototypes. There is a cloud storm of dust left in our cab ride's wake. I reach for my red bandana to tie around my neck, mouth, and nose for protection against the toxic particulates no doubt catching in the air.

We stop. There are traces of housing along the road, but it's eerily quiet as we approach the coordinates Miranda gave me. I wait for the dust cloud to pass us before rolling my window down. The open woundedness—Anzaldúa's apt description of the border persists—comes to life as we catch sight of the structures's tops on the other side of the fence. We get out of the car and stand on our tippy toes, trying to look past the corrugated fence and into the country we left behind that morning. I look around to see what can help elevate us. I find an old tractor tire that Michelle holds steady. We three try for a better, longer look. Then we meet Jorge.

Jorge, a short and wiry man in his early thirties, pops out of his shanty wearing a sunbeaten black baseball cap, a dusty gray T-shirt and loose Levi's. The cheery smile on his mouth, the familiar lilt reminding me of my aunts in San Salvador. After we tell him why we're here, he brings out a short, wooden ladder. *Gracias, paisano.* I tell him my mom is from El Salvador, too, as I offer him some money and a meek smile.

I hold on to the top of the border fence, the one initiated in the Clinton-era Operation Gatekeeper and secured during the Bush years. It runs along the line through Baja California into the Sea of Cortez; its rusty bars even spill into the Pacific Ocean. I'm trying to tread lightly in hopes that the rusty metal digging into the flesh of my hands won't break skin as I stabilize my footing on the ladder.

Once I get a clear sight line of the prototypes, I feel the impact of their power immediately, along with the ache of my family's history, of all they risked to arrive and to stay in the U.S., risks echoed in the caravan of migrants seeking asylum today. As structures, the prototypes are a chorus of intimidation, shoulder to shoulder, their lines so clean and so out of touch with the elements immediately surrounding us. The hues chosen for each prototype make some gesture to the parched terrain—the desert sand and walnut brown—as well as hues of sky and concrete and the shining line where the two meet. These are shades and shapes that invite a sharp contrast to Tijuana's palette of abject poverty. The prototypes look as though they could cut right through you.

But I can't flee or fight from the top of this rickety ladder. I stand there and hold my ground and keep my eyes steady and dare to imagine what's next on the horizon that these things obfuscate. Taking it all in—the valley, the fences that make accessing the prototypes from the U.S. side impossible, the fence I'm supporting myself on—I suddenly see what the critics saw. Any one of these prototypes could have easily been created by one of the masters of minimalism. Not Donald Trump, but rather Donald Judd.

———

The original border fence, a sturdy stretch of corrugated metal colorfully graffitied with NO MUROS and HECHO EN MEXICO, becomes a line disappearing into a rising vanishing point into a deeper, more mysterious Mexico. Standing on the arbitrary line itself brings to light the failure of what borders are supposed to do—keep people in and keep people out. (This even though the migrants' labor, siphoned almost from vein and artery, bodies spirited away from family and alienated from ancestral land, has led both nations to look the other way, turn away from the border, for so long.) I imagine those who've never had to risk anything to get here looking through the fence, watching as bodies are dramatically subjugated into the maquiladoras, a ghost ship of capitalist production.

There it is—Trump's "beautiful" wall. Signed off on, however uneasily, as the land art of a fascist state. As critic Jerry Saltz wrote, like "minimalism, these prototypes are hard-edged geometry and impervious materials brought into the

American landscape of the West and arranged to impose order, inspire awe, and try to manage and align mystic political forces." Just like the land in Owens Valley, California, got caught between policy and prisoners at Manzanar.[13] Just like Heart Mountain outside Ralston, Wyoming.[14] I feel caught in the border's entropic crosshairs. Here, it is easy to read the markings left on the earth by the necrocapitalist superpowers of the post-NAFTA world. Here are eight examples of what one wall could do to "secure a border." Eight models for keeping us from each other.

History, I think, as we all stand silent for a moment, is the manual, and Jorge, Manuel, Michelle, and I—we borderland denizens from both sides of this wall—await its future directives. Michelle and I say good-bye to Jorge and Manuel, walk back out through customs and onward to the lot where I parked my truck.

———

Seeing each prototype was like going to a trade show for someone's fixer-upper, a flipped house waiting for its gentrification fence to be painted a tasteful neutral, for its colors to cohere despite its location (but anticipating that the value in that location would rise); would this mythical wall match the sky or usher in a new era of concrete-minded futurity? Or would it be the color of a grassland caught in a perpetual drought? Would this manifestation of power be distilled into a miniature

---

13. National Park Service, "Japanese Americans at Manzanar," https://www.nps.gov/manz/learn/historyculture/japanese-americans-at-manzanar.htm.

14. Steven Blingo, "A Brief History of Heart Mountain Relocation Center," Wyoming State Historical Society, November 8, 2014, https://www.wyohistory.org/encyclopedia/brief-history-heart-mountain-relocation-center.

version, sold in the living room section of Design Within Reach? Tasteful studio partitions in eight styles? Not when the Trump administration was seeking nearly $18 billion from Congress to extend and reinforce a border wall with Mexico. Not when Trump was holding 800,000 federal workers economically hostage with the longest government shutdown ever. Not when a Democratic House was digging in its heels to avoid giving in any further to his madness. A monumental manifestation and it will be beautiful. But can beauty move beyond a clean line? Can minimalism's compulsory privileged position as a default marking of artistic integrity be reconsidered?

———

I can't remember where I read of Donald Judd's assertion that his work would be more meaningful if it were placed somewhere more permanent. I think of the ghosts that roam the halls of these assertions. Judd, whom art critic Roberta Smith eulogized as "one of the foremost American artists of the postwar era and a major figure in the Minimal Art movement," no doubt found the cleanliness of the wide, open space at Marfa, Texas, in line with his vision built on the fealty to "specific objects"—the boxes, the stacks, the repetition of true phenomenological things that ultimately lead back to the box and its variations. If only the environment could hold the meaning of his assertions without taking into account its own temporary ontology, as erosion and water shortages are more than mere material reminders of environmental limitations. In addition, how can we think of Judd's concrete structures that dot the landscape of his Chinati Foundation as permanent when it sits butt-to-butt with the Border Patrol headquarters off the stretch of Highway 90 that enters and exits Marfa. I've been to Marfa and have walked the beaten paths that run parallel to the concrete structures that make the town an arts destination for lovers of land art. It's hard for me to completely corroborate Judd's desire for the work to simply be interesting. What's interesting to me is the way history is forced off the land along with most of its inhabitants, a historical awareness I'm supposed to check at the door once I put the red Chinati sticker on my lapel. I wouldn't want to sully my experience.

But then again, a new thirty-foot border wall—distilled in equal measure from the design minds of Chinati and Border Patrol agents—sits sixty miles from Marfa in Ojinaga, Chihuahua. That's close enough for a day trip: another art-tourist destination, perhaps.

———

The running loop in my head in the days, weeks, months after my visit takes on the aspect of a codependent relationship. *Aren't you tired of an established aesthetic that pulsates well enough through toxic spectacles to occasionally penetrate the discerning sensibilities of American art critics? Haven't you encountered the difficulty that comes with forging a relationship with art, a bid for rightful representation, time and time again? How many times have you learned and mastered art's parlances only to be caught off guard by new regimes and attending social conditions that sever you from the language of art in the first place? You accept helpless dogs exploited on a looped video in the Guggenheim or long queues to see Marina render millennials into salty puddles on a concrete MoMA floor. You get called an art-washing vendido. But you stay. Sometimes you stay and watch your friend's four-hour durational performance in front of the local county jail, other times you stay in even more precarious terrains, daring to thrive on a land turned state where you are surveilled and further conditioned against your own instinct.*

Art is a hostile place.

In its own attempts to build monuments to itself, art literally builds fences. Some of us still make it through, cracking the obstacle course with aplomb either as practitioners or interlocutors. Many don't. *Still, the prototypes were a shock you should have seen coming—their hostility doesn't exist in a void.* It's there for a reason. And arming itself with the relentless shock of the now is a good a reason for the art world to ride out and leverage the frightening moment trapping us all.

Declaring eight border wall prototypes as land art: an artbro provocation. A didacticism of trolling or the trolling of didacticism. Still, while these new, insidious monuments rise, older monuments are brought down by individuals working across difference and conceptual execution. Bree Newsome's act of civil disobedience lit us up when she was arrested for removing the Confederate flag from the South Carolina state house grounds.[15] Or Therese Patricia Okoumou's Statue of Liberty sit-in protesting the separation of migrant families at the border on the Fourth of July.[16] Several contemporary city governments eagerly marching toward the progressive horizon do so literally in the middle of the night, as happened with the disappearing racist statues in Baltimore, where four

---

15. "#KeepItDown Confederate Flag Takedown," https://www.youtube.com/watch?v=gr-mt1P94cQ.

16. Victoria Bekiempis, "Woman Who Climbed Statue of Liberty in Immigration Protest Found Guilty," *Guardian,* December 17, 2018, https://www.theguardian.com/us-news/2018/dec/17/statue-of-liberty-climber-trial-us-immigration.

Confederate monuments were dismantled a week after the white nationalist rally in Charlottesville.[17]

And yet the wall prototypes were the surprise we didn't know we needed. A metaphor so brutally obvious. A brutalist movement revived by a populace's desire for an art inching closer to an open identification with fascism. An antagonized reminder of history repeating all over itself, the border an exhausted hamster wheel, a Sisyphean crossing where migrants are only ever seen as laborers if they are seen at all. *What else can we squeeze out of the border?* You stop asking yourself how art could be involved in a fascist project. *Art has never left its side.*

———

I am famished by the time we pass through the border checkpoint at Otay Mesa. As soon as we get back to Chula Vista, Michelle and I stop for some amazing carne asada tacos, deep fried quesadillas, and Mineraguas. The tacos were equal parts spirit cleanser and spicy meat fix, since our friend Ceci's wedding is offering guests vegetarian fare. But it felt good to be in a space of sensory and familiar pleasure. Couples bickering and their children squealing at the tables and red vinyl booths around us, the speakers in the strip mall taqueria blaring the latest reggaeton. We could eat and we could enjoy ourselves, be reminded that there was so much of ourselves still capable of bringing and feeling joy even as each new day and week with the Trump administration meant something unimaginably

---

17. Jamie Grierson, "Baltimore Takes Down Confederate Statues in Middle of Night," *Guardian,* August 16, 2017, https://www.theguardian.com/us-news/2017/aug/16/baltimore-takes-down-confederate-statues-in-middle-of-night.

nefarious coming to fruition. A sensate for the improbable. If we lost our joy then we had lost everything. If we could keep our families together for one day, we might as well revel in the ephemeral and hope we could still summon the memory.

They want our tacos but they don't want us, I sing-sang in a familiar protest rhythm between bites. I savored every bite of roasted green onions, cilantro, and smoky chipotle red sauce. *But that was true before a wall.* We want so desperately to belong to ourselves that we still await liberation through representation. And the cultural zeitgeist put that burden of recognition on whomever could master narrating the democratizing logics of the taco for a public bummed out by the xenophobics in D.C.

Son capaz. Michelle is right. They're capable of extracting even the food we make from us behind the barriers—whether they're the ones in Otay Mesa or the points that connect the stitches between here and Brownsville and Matamoros, the points of land that kiss the Pacific on the West, with the Sea of Cortez in the middle and the Gulf of Mexico at the end of the demarcation.

I drive Michelle back to her sister's house and head to my three-star discount app hotel room in Pacific Beach, a little neighborhood south of La Jolla in San Diego, to get ready. We would meet back up again for the wedding. It feels strange to pull out my suit, though it is the suit of my dreams—charcoal gray sharkskin. I blew my grant money getting it tailored to my short and stocky butch body, even though I bought it for ten dollars a decade prior. It feels good to lay it on the crisp white comforter that makes my hotel bed look like a cloud. I want to crawl under the bedding though. I have it pretty cushy, considering where I would lay my frayed nerves for the night, which reminds me of the way mobility works for anyone with a U.S. passport. If I had more time, I could soak my feet in the tub. Instead I pull my black socks and black brogues out of my weekender bag. I feel more awake, ready to be social, once I am out of the shower and have buttoned up my white shirt. I pull out a gray tie, then a red one, and finally decide to go white on white. It feels strange to see myself fill the suit out handsomely when my synapses are firing off rounds. I am abuzz with fear and fury as if I've spent the last few hours chain-smoking one hundred cigarettes. I step out of my room into the parking lot to collect my truck and feel the bay breeze on my gooseskin. I feel overdressed walking past everyone at the resort hotel wearing swim trunks and suits, children in an array of inflatables around their limbs and bodies. I am off to see people I haven't seen in twenty years—aging punks from San Diego, the nihilist crème de la late nineties post-hardcore crème, a screamo-emo scene carved out by this fellowship of misanthropes. This day was dedicated to reuniting with those with whom I built my tastes for dissonance and off-time signatures alongside the anarcho-politics that roared against a state building walls for people and dropping trade regulations.

———

In 1994 I was eighteen with a bullet, aching to see any live punk rock any chance I could get. And I did. By then my parents had long accepted that my mode of resistance meant not seeing me most weekends while I stood in the periphery of the mosh pit for any Rocket from the Crypt shows happening from Westwood to Tijuana. That summer Ceci, Torie, and I would drive south on I-5 to catch San Diego emo-billy faves doing a secret show at Ché Café. The Ché Café continues to be a worker co-operative, gathering space, and live music venue located on the University of California San Diego campus in La Jolla, California. Its exteriors are decked out in murals of Ché Guevara, Rigoberta Menchú, Karl Marx, and Angela Davis, and it has hosted every emo band that ever mattered to me. Everyone's played there. Even Los Angeles' own Rage against the Machine, when they were on Columbia Records, would do secret sets for the homies from Zack de la Rocha's Inside Out straightedge days. Everyone loves the Ché Café. Even de la Rocha described it as "a place that is not only a great venue, but a source of inspiration and community-building for any artist, student, or worker that has entered its doors." The Ché has a storied reputation as a place where any revolutionary can grab a hummus sandwich, much to UC San Diego's chagrin. To keep university officials off their scent, the café has signage that reads "C.H.E.—Cheap, Healthy Eats."

San Diego in the early nineties had a vibrant underground of punk musicians who had learned their instruments well enough to start innovating on the genres that birthed them. It was punk but it was melodic. It was melodic but it was also relentlessly erratic. It was chaotic but it was also pertinent to my long nights of contemplation during those early days of one-dollar-gallon-gas road trips back home from San Diego. One of the most noteworthy bands emblematic of the "San Diego Sound" was Antioch Arrow. They toured their brand of minute-long songs up and down the West Coast, stopping one sweaty San Fernando Valley afternoon in northeast Los Angeles to play a storage garage someone had turned into a DIY venue. Antioch Arrow stopped in to see if they could open for my other favorite band, Los Crudos, from Chicago. As soon as Antioch Arrow turned up the knobs on their Marshall stacks, all you heard were the frenetic guitar wailing and snare drum slapping, and all you saw were human spinning tops wilding out like dirty white boy blurs on a Van Gogh canvas.

Us Los Angeles kids were hooked. We started wearing high water Levi's Sta-Prest jeans and white studded leather belts, and combing down our hair like Dr. Spock from *Star Trek*. And I started to follow that band around, which meant finding myself often in the strange beach underground that was San Diego. Antioch Arrow broke up two years later, but the members started other bands that I wanted to see. And San Diego was a scene I wanted to belong to, although I would never admit that to anyone in Los Angeles. It was easy enough to get down there with Ceci, who was soon my roommate in a two-bedroom in a neighborhood that she called Echo Park and I called Silver Lake. We were right on the border and anyone who came over always argued which side of the line we lived on back in 1998. I'd come home some days from my weird digital music label in Santa Monica to invitations from Ceci to head to San Diego to see a band play.

I'm too tired, dude.

Don't ever let your job dictate your life.

. . . Fine, let's go.

Ceci and I both loved the music, the scene, gathering together around the sketchiest of locales in the alleys and surf shacks of San Diego, pounding Tecates with the locals while the Pacific pounded the shore. But she enjoyed hanging out with those young men in ways I didn't, and they ended up becoming closer to her than to me. This was back when she used to rock a horn on her head, greased up with Royal Crown that made her look like a girl Ed Grimley. She eventually moved to San Diego after finishing up law school in Los Angeles to practice housing advocacy for numerous projects working with the homeless.

————

I leave my hotel and drive down the main drag with Sail Bay to my left and Fiesta Bay to my right. It's stunning. But I realize I could probably never afford to live in this, the Southern California of postcards. I park my dusty truck half a mile from the Women's Rowing Club in a Pacific Beach neighborhood with Spanish-style mansions and multilevel Craftsman bungalows and hope I don't break a sweat under the bright sun getting to the venue. Just as I start to saunter my way to the sidewalk, I hear a raspy-voiced charlatan call out my name—or my punk rock name, that is.

Is that you, Rocky? I turn around and see the old bastard himself. Isreal has a distinct growl that shoves itself into an earworm every time I drive through Pomona, California. He was the singer for a band called Man Is the Bastard and a difficult figure in that nineties scene, so seeing him with a full paunch, a five o'clock shadow of strawberry-blond fuzz on his face, and a ratty, thin glen-plaid blazer gives me pause for the ways relational dynamics shift as we age. I feel my shoulders relax as he comes in for a warm hug. He is a sweet man, glowing with an aura soaked in pain, wounded in all of the obvious ways. Ours was a generation forced to stiffen our lips, deny our needs for nurturance, and wing it when dropped in the oceans of intimacy with no recourse. We were red flags waiting to be set on fire.

Oh shit, Loomis Slovak? That was the name of his other band when Man Is the Bastard temporarily kicked him out. *How long has it been? Last time I saw you we were both flirting with sobriety at the House of Pies. Where's your partner?*

Oh man, I saw you at the beginning of that relationship. Well, two kids later and a move to Temecula, she's decided she wants to divorce me. He says it with a grimace, and then I grimace.

Well, shit, you got two really cute kids out of it. And now we're at a wedding!

He shrugs. *Well, I'm flying solo. Let's wingman each other tonight, yeah?*

We arrive together and put IPAs in each other's hands for the rest of the afternoon until Ceci and her seven-year-old come down the aisle. I tell him what took me to Tucson and he tells me that his wife resented him for robbing her of her lesbianism.

If memory serves me well, Sarah wasn't your first queer rodeo, Iz.

————

I start to load up on chips and guacamole and peek inside the rowing club, glimpsing quaint oil paintings of sailing superyachts hanging on wood paneled walls, when I see another ghost in the form of Patrick Delaney, who I hadn't seen since our trip to Havana in 1999. We had gone to a young communist gathering on the ills of neoliberalism and globalization, bunking in dormitories that would wake up all the international inhabitants by blasting Silvio Rodriguez at seven in the morning. Pat and I were there mostly to hang out with Ceci and Torie, who were the politics punks. But I first encountered Pat on Los Angeles's public radio airwaves. He used to host the afternoon show on KXLU that was my audio lifeline to bands like Fugazi and Alice Donut as well as to more experimental bands that studied punk like Slug or Laughing Hyenas from Chicago. His show gave me new ears for a world I was ready to inhabit, a world away from the Huntington Park that claimed me in a Catholic school uniform for many years. Of course Pat and I are tag teaming deejay duties for the wedding party once the ceremony and dinner portions of the evening are complete. I try to get him to play more cumbia for the bride's Mexican side, but he is set on playing from deep in the crates.

I run into Torie and her husband, Anthony, and their vivacious five-year-old, Inez, who I hosted last August in Tucson during one of the desert's hotter summers on record. I run into Leilani, who I hadn't seen since the Free Mumia march we went to in San Francisco in 1998. And Nessa from Whittier, who every brown punk boy was in love with in 1998, and her daughters, who are her teenage mini-mes. I run into Quetzal and Martha and catch up on the local L.A. beef between curators of Chicano art and the artists whose precious archives they couldn't penetrate, and the anarchist, polyamorous Fran with her new girlfriend. Monogamy—they are trying it out. I run into San Diego native daughter Maribel, who was Pat Delaney's first girlfriend at twenty-three, and her white boo, Paul, who flew down from Portland. We were all late bloomers and sexuality was second to our music scenes. I run into so many great faces, all of whom hear about my visit to the border wall prototypes and my purpose for visiting them. Every conversation is meant to offer a brief history of land art as well as an anecdote about my personal interest. Or vendetta against it. The conflicted appreciation. The flurry of feelings that keeps dust deviling out of my mouth with each new IPA I swig. I am butchsplaining my ass off. And in every conversation I see the glint of panic.

These aging punks, stuffing shaved corn salad and roasted zucchini into their mouths and washing it down with Chardonnay, chasing the kids from their blended families around the wedding cake table, narrating every Drive Like Jehu show they ever attended and the time their eyes were pummeled by pepper spray at the 2000 Democratic National Convention in Los Angeles, showing off the Rocket from the

Crypt tattoos that earned them free entry to every show until the apocalypse, never imagining things would get worse than Bush stealing the election or Halliburton siphoning every drop of oil out of Iraq or the invasion of Afghanistan in the name of nation-building.

I see Michelle again, this time wearing a form-fitting red cotton dress that makes her look like the dancing-lady emoji. She looks great. We both do, considering we came back covered in maquila toxins and border fence dust. I give her a look that says, *Can you believe we did that?* But she doesn't respond in the same way. She is ready to dance her troubles away. Or to at least dance with her troubles. It's a good coping mechanism. We would be in trouble for at least two more years.

Art in the Time of Art-Washing

2018 | I was back at the Redz Bar of my queer adolescence, a pang of grief gnawing in my gut. The establishment had closed its doors in 2015, after more than fifty years as one of the few spaces in East Los Angeles for Chicana lesbians to congregate in conviviality. Redz, which reopened in late 2016, continues to be important to me, and I wanted to recognize its historic role in providing that crucial space by organizing an evening featuring the filmic works of Oakland-based artist Xandra Ibarra. The event marked my return to the bar under its new ownership.

I pulled out two barstools from right in the middle of the counter and looked up to see the familiar sight of vinyl records glued to the ceiling. Red vinyl, yellow vinyl, blue vinyl, black. I had arrived early with my friend Thea, a curator at a small Seattle gallery and my best femme friend, who was eager to see Boyle Heights up close and personally. We had stopped for the world-famous bean and cheese burritos with green sauce from Al & Bea's and parked ourselves in the middle of the late afternoon crowd of butch-femme regulars, who were decked out head to toe in Dodgers gear, digging into their buckets of icy cold Coronas. Thea and I stuck out a bit—me in a white and neon-flourished Hawaiian shirt and short green shorts, Thea in the monochromatic angularity of Eileen Fisher. The evening was my fourth and final program for the 2018 *Dirty Looks: On Location*, a film and performance series that was the brainchild of my friend, the film curator Bradford Nordeen.[18] Bradford had knighted a handful of artists, programmers, impresarios, and deejays into event conveners. We organized a muscular monthlong series that gave neighborhood bars throughout Los Angeles their moment under the queer historical and vernacular sun. I chose Ibarra's work because of the way it resonates with Redz history in addressing the queer and colonial histories that brought Mexicans from El Paso to East L.A. throughout the twentieth century. The event was my attempt to tether the two cities, an umbilical cord that queers a history of Mexican migration following the Mexican Revolution.

Ten years earlier I would have felt good, in an uncomplicated way, about the program's intent and execution. Ten years earlier, I was scraping by with an administrative university job that had been cut down to seventeen hours after the 2008 crash. That job only existed because of an endowment, and when Wall Street's down so is gender and women's studies. Now, I couldn't help but think I was setting myself up for a callout, given the current political wariness of artists in a Boyle Heights I hadn't lived in since 2010. The neighborhood was burdened by a housing crisis reaching its boiling point, and intimidation tactics like doxxing were standard practice in Boyle Heights, which had become somehow alienated by Chicanx art—not the Chicanx art championed by the late Sister Karen Boccalero (often credited as the founder of the organization Self-Help Graphics & Art[19]) but not *not*

---

18. https://dirtylooksla.org/

19. https://www.selfhelpgraphics.com/

championed either; this was an art that had become the nouveau signal of a Boyle Heights in transition. An art by Chicanx artists who took flight into and out of prestigious BFA and MFA programs and returned to a neighborhood that was once the epicenter for Japanese migrants who came to L.A. en masse after the 1906 San Francisco earthquake, followed in the twenties and thirties by Jewish Eastern Europeans. Art changed these neighborhoods. Artists were telling stories many were starving to hear. Sometimes I feel like Tomás Ybarra-Frausto never should have given us the theory of rasquachismo because once you have language to describe the representational depth of beauty of the harsh places we come from, those in power want to take it away. Our historical imprints enhance the value of a neighborhood. Our histories sell, whereas our lives obstruct profits.

My anxiety was new and had emerged in response to an unusual Instagram message I received in the fall of 2017: my Latinx identity, or so I gleaned from this message, was being coopted by a Boyle Heights gallery to push out low-income renters from their Boyle Heights apartments. *Who is this?* I hissed to myself. I was struck by social media's ability to make me feel like it was always already instantaneously omnipotent and omniscient and that I was in trouble. But I get that information has become the currency in the democratization of surveillance and that's what our little smartphones enable— our surveillance of one another. It's also really dramatic. But sometimes it inspires dialogue, and gossip and critique are a powerful combination. Gossip queers critique. And I will never begrudge a good callout.

I texted Pau, a young Chicanx who lived in nearby Highland Park but was raised in the California high desert community of Hesperia. Pau was my friend and the curator of the exhibition in question. They were one of the hardest-working artists I knew and explained that the main person behind the incendiary Instagram account was a white trans art bro whose wealth was publicly known, an organizer who had fallen out with members of his cohort who had recently opened a new gallery in Boyle Heights; the gallery was backed by New York investors, inspiring necessary scrutiny. I took a minute to let that information assimilate in my mind. It all felt so wildly imagined. But these details were part of an anecdotal register permeating a Los Angeles arts community struggling to make sense of the stain of art-washing (arts organizations helping scrub the stink of gentrification from developers seizing upon real estate opportunities). The accuracies are what we lose in the constant, unrelenting discourse anchored in perception and optics. Or what happens when no one interfaces in person anymore.

I had never heard of the anonymous Instagram account critical of many Latinx artists making art about East Los Angeles in East Los Angeles. Naming these identity markers of the caller is important. It's how a politic of identity gets determined. The caller used these declarative callouts as a strategy, a provocation: as a mean-spirited critique of the artists' "authentic Latinidad" as if the whole thing isn't just made up to preserve proximities to whiteness and power. But it's true some of the artists had one non-Latinx parent, others were probably trust-funded or were just "too white" to even be considered "real" Latinxs. No one in that exhibition was trust-funded to my knowledge, but that isn't even the point.

That callout felt like we were being asked to show our papers.

It was effective in some ways. Some of the artists haven't shown since that episode, which played out mostly on social media. Having their identities leveraged in a public and virulent way has startled them into an anxious silence. Several of my friends and acquaintances had liked the image, a doom-scrolled admission of their approval on a timeline no one stops to contemplate anymore, I thought.

How could Chicanx artists make work without somehow engaging a Chicanx epicenter?

I lurked on the account to see a post calling out my old friend Tanya Saracho, showrunner for *Vida* (which, according to its website, is a dramedy series "about two Mexican-American siblings from East Los Angeles"), for selling out Boyle Heights. She is referred to as a *whitetina*.

Was I a whitetina? Or a whitetinx, to remain congruent to my old-school bulldagger swagger with new-school queer theory presentation? Why wasn't I called a leva (short for *levantado*, a name reserved for someone who is elevated or uppity)? Was my desire to move slowly above my station—a glacially paced social mobility—a problem? Was asking to get paid for a performance a problem? Was wanting what I was owed a problem?

Space in a community as a contributing member: I dreamed of a rightful place at the family dinner table. Permission, when necessary, to be a loving gadfly.

I was living in Tucson at the time of the callout and had to think about how a poem of mine could be capable of aiding and abetting community displacement when I myself had to leave a northeast Los Angeles neighborhood to improve my lot in what was heretofore a broke queer life. I knew displacement well, even as I was often contacted for work about queerness, brownness, and how the two intersect in an ever-changing L.A. landscape. I had been asked to include my poem in the small publication for *Facing,* a show focused on Latinx portraiture at the artist-run gallery BBQLA, a space whose controversy was new to me. Timo Fahler, son of an Oklahoma Chicana with El Paso roots, is one of two guys I know who runs BBQLA, and I liked and trusted him enough to agree to participate. We had hung out in Marfa the previous summer, both of us in collaborative efforts with our mutual friend, rafa esparza. About four artists had pulled their work before *Facing* opened, in response to the Instagram callout. Some may have done so in fear of retribution or in solidarity with local low-income residents at risk of being displaced. There were empty spaces on some of the BBQLA walls, a gesture making visible the choices of each artist. The opening, which I attended, served freshly smoked brisket and coleslaw and cornbread for free.

How to briefly illustrate a brown life in the arts? Many of us arrive to art from origins that register in most narratives as humble beginnings—that is, our parents emerged from an immigrant underclass that has beaten the odds. If you can buy a home a decade after being paid to take care of children twenty-four seven at fifty dollars a week during your first four years in a new country then you, my friend, have beaten the odds. Which is what makes our histories appealing—the raw underdoggedness of needing to survive is thrilling to consume from a safe distance. These stories are the discursive equivalents of a cockfight.

And so we, the children of those who have ascended successfully to the middle classes, move toward the arts as a promise of sustainability beyond survival. We make an art that calls on the ancestors who survived encroachment and expulsion, disaster and disease. We tell their stories through our own. We stitch a story about where we are from to make up for the history seized from us. Our stories navigate gatekeeping strategies from institutions as diverse as university art programs, local nonprofits, galleries, and museums. Our stories make it to the other side of those gates. But now we may have been intercepted by a new level of financialization. How to make art and a life that isn't influenced by market forces, or that is able to operate outside of exploited labor and toxic consumption? How to leave our art behind when some of us are told that our artistic projects are putting poorer people in jeopardy? We are forming identities in need of empowerment through expression while trying to arrive at answers that could satisfy similarly circumstanced detractors (even those who owned homes in these neighborhoods). Most of us had been priced out of apartments once a lease agreement came to a close. No one owed us anything and yet we had a right to be there.

Who knew a Latinx immigrant middle class could exist, only to quickly be undercut by a government that values its corporations more than its citizenry?

My parents were part of that class, which meant a modest mortgage in southeast Los Angeles and sunrise drives to see the dentist in Tijuana. They met at El Mercadito on 3rd and Lorena in the early seventies, when my mom lived in a spartan one-bedroom in the Estrada Courts housing project. My dad a Mexicano from Pachuca, Hidalgo, working at a pressing plant in Vernon, and Mom, a Salvadoran woman barely making it by doing piecework as a seamstress downtown. I was born at the county hospital before it became USC Medical Center in Lincoln Heights—before USC offered its employees a housing purchase subsidy starting at $20,000 to buy homes in neighborhoods like Lincoln Heights and the South Central communities surrounding the main university campus. I was baptized at Our Lady Queen of Angels across the street from the old Plaza Olvera Street, and I grew up in Huntington Park and Bell Gardens. I saw Vaginal Creme Davis open for the Voluptuous Horror of Karen Black when I was seventeen, playing in bands and palling around with the Yao sisters from Emily's Sassy Lime, the other teenage girls of color in that Jabberjaw milieu that later contributed to various underground cultures. Over a span of fifteen years, I have lived in Silver Lake, Echo Park, Lincoln Heights, and Montecito Heights. I found my first community outside of my immediate family at Bienestar Human Services in East L.A. on Beverly Boulevard, in the form of support group meetings for Latina lesbians. I learned about collectives and made zines and organized showcases for Black and brown queer and woman-identified emerging artists hungry to connect with one another. We only had access to places like Highways Performance Space in Santa Monica, an organization that was eager to bring our voices to its black box theater. The Westside welcomed us. In fact, I never had a gig in East Los Angeles during the entire time I performed with Butchlalis de Panochtitlan.

Here's my proof. These are my papers. May my agitators approve my history.

These are just experiences I had as a younger person, and certainly not shields from the critique my current middle-aged actions inspired. But the struggle to ethically express oneself under the conditions of late capitalism was present. As someone who spent the first decade of the twentieth century finding my voice under the globalized violence of the idiocracy that was the Bush Jr. administration, it wouldn't occur to me that things could get worse. I was an innocent who wanted to present my work in the communities that raised me—East Los Angeles, from the north to the southeast of the Los Angeles River. But presenting venues were few except for Josefina López's Casa 0101, a tiny black box that did everything to support emerging theater artists. But I wasn't a theater artist. I was into performance art and Brechtian approaches to narrative.

It took a series of turnstile changes in these neighborhoods to make room for organizations with missions to present work by queer brown and Black artists, particularly those with roots in these communities. These callouts tend to reify the torment of Latinx queers (many of them children of Mexican and Central American immigrants), whose initial response as residents of these neighborhoods is to flee.

Flight had always been my instinct.

These were the conditions that underscored my attempts at eking out a creative life, working in arts nonprofit organizations and universities as a low-tiered administrator. I moved out of Los Angeles and into a San Francisco housing fray that saw me move three times in a year. I had landed a job as a community arts curator at one of San Francisco's larger arts institutions that had received over half a million in funding to do community-based projects in South of Market (SoMa), the Mission District, and parts of Oakland. I have lived the contradictions before what we saw happen in Boyle Heights. I moved four times in five years and each time put me deeper into a debt I still contend with daily. That financial stress was a bonding rite with other artists and nonprofit workers who were living collectively just to be able to live.

Mine might not be the Molotov-cocktail instigations of a radical militant, but I can be counted on to model other ontological possibilities for younger artists-in-the-making who benefit from mentorship and continued dialogue in spaces that want us to be there. I'm not calling for civility, even as I struggle to understand how white artists who use social practice to support a sector of the community that is inarguably living in precarious conditions might then turn around and suggest that the emerging Latinx artists they have taught in their art school classes and have shared exhibition space with should be met with vitriol. A simple desire instilled in many Latinx children of immigrants is to improve the circumstances that condition a life under capitalism. That often requires some of us to endure the violent professionalization that comes with higher educational institutions, including learning from masters of relational aesthetics (and agreeing to their logics that what we do is called community art). We have to leave behind the parts of our respective rasquachismo matrices in order to learn about rasquachismo from the vantage point of the departmental chair. We have to learn about the workers from the bosses.

———

Perhaps the hardest part of reckoning with our Latinx artist identity is thinking about historical repetition—or how we come for one another as a way to fend off being come for ourselves. Living in Arizona forced me into the historical fact of the intra-ethnic violence Mexicans inflicted on the Apache and Yaqui in the name of state-building. This is a truth that runs parallel to Mexicans fleeing the Revolution of 1910—its violence created many Angelenxs with El Pasoan roots. Xandra Ibarra is from El Paso and her work charges the connections between her city and mine—their borderlands and their histories of colonization—through a queer, often provocative, lens. It's important for Ibarra's work to be shown in Redz Bar, a lesbian bar that opened in the late fifties and catered primarily to queer, working-class Chicanas. It's important for those conceptual bridges to emerge between those who live in Boyle Heights and those in exile from the embattled neighborhood. However, sometimes bridging means that the good-intentioned white friends living and lurking in our networks are the ones who can afford to remain in these neighborhoods. When artists and organizers (like me) present the optics of these events to those white friends it situates those of us (like me) who lie in the political liminality as champions of the marginalized subject and brokers of the white gaze.

Is this what moving beyond survival looks like? Does it mean losing some semblance of a self constituted through surviving the racist policies that structure how we inhabit contested publics—whether it's receiving a subpar primary and secondary education, a predatory loan, or speaking in Spanish at the chain restaurant in a better-resourced adjacent neighborhood? Some might say I choose this loss and that doing so requires a selling out. Do I sell out so you don't have to? In 2013 I worked for an institution that played its own role in displacing a local community under duress; approximately four thousand people in the SoMa area were pushed out to make room for the Yerba Buena Center for the Arts and SFMOMA. Various lawsuits challenged dislocation, financing, and environmental concerns, including the successful 1970–1973 Tenants and Owners in Opposition to Redevelopment (TOOR) suit, which emerged over the relocation process and halted development, though not permanently.[20] It's easy to critique these development endeavors when they're elsewhere, not where one lives, relies on for rent money, or longs to return. When it's your old neighborhood, you have to stop and wonder how your complicity persists even when brown bodies—our brown bodies together—are regarded with more suspicion when navigating the sociopathic capitalist regime than are those whose

20. This is chronicled in David Woo's 2017 University of San Francisco dissertation titled *People, Land, and Profit in the South of Market: A Critical Analysis of the Central SoMa Plan.*

careers arrived on the backs of the same brown bodies they proclaim to engage.

Others will argue that these are exactly the opportunities our families risked their lives for when coming north for a better life. And that's the problem. *Queriamos norte.*

SECTION III

LA MANO
OBRA

Vessel Among Vessels:
Laura Aguilar's Body in Landscape

2018 | Laura Aguilar, the photographer and chronicler of brown life who centered lesbians and her own fat body, passed away in April 2018 in Southern California. Her death from complications from diabetes was untimely, beset with tragedy. Diabetes, which is possible though not easy to reverse, reminds us of a U.S. healthcare system that brings into relief the depths of precarity to which Chicana artists, intellectuals, and cultural producers endure and succumb. Aguilar died from the same conditions that took Gloria Anzaldúa, the philosopher poet from the Rio Grande Valley in South Texas whose feminist theories of the borderlands envisaged a new "mestiza consciousness" emerging in response to the psychic wounds of colonial encounters and occupation. Anzaldúa's philosophies of Chicana consciousness center on simultaneous awareness of and resistance to oppression, what literary theorist María Lugones describes as "the possibility of resistance revealed in the perceiving of the self in the process of being oppressed as another face of the self in the process of resisting oppression." That conceptual ouroboros, the snake that eats its own tail, is metabolized in Aguilar's Nature series, where the photographer centers her own body in the desert. Her images are a quiet insurrection against policing engines that power the landscape, along with histories of violence against the Indigenous and Mexican people and otherwise marginalized bodies.

In *Nature Self-Portrait #14* (1996), Aguilar's body lays in side view within a bantam-sized landscape, with her hand on the reflective surface of a natural spring of water, enacting both Echo and Narcissus in her gaze. Aguilar as both subject and observer sets ablaze the Anzaldúan concept of *nepantla:* a "space in-between, the locus and sign of transition" that exists in the creative act as the "place/space where realities interact and imaginative shifts happen."

In 1992, Aguilar, herself a Chicana lesbian, experienced an imaginative shift in her practice. She was so taken with the Plush Pony, a bar in East L.A. that catered predominantly to working-class Chicana lesbians, that she set up her camera and offered to take portraits of the locals as a way to socially lubricate what was an otherwise difficult scene for Aguilar, a shy self-identified introvert, to navigate. A very butch-femme joint, the Plush Pony was a space where Aguilar found some sense of kin with its barflies—enough to immortalize them in her now infamous Plush Pony series. Because its clientele was perhaps rougher than the usual ilk that frequented bars like the Palms or the Normandie Room in the West Hollywood of the eighties and nineties, the Plush Pony differed from the normative spectatorship that Aguilar had grown weary of appealing to. The lawyers, activists, artists, and academics she had previously photographed in her Latina Lesbians series were an echelon ready for its respectability close-up. In the portrait series encapsulating the years 1985 to 1991, we meet the subjects by name, accompanied by a lyrical caption summarizing their aspirations come to fruition. Carla, for example, in a sexy black motorcycle jacket, her voluminously coiffed bangs brushing the corner of her forehead like a Chicana Fonz, looks into the camera to emphasize her tenacity, which is corroborated by the text: "my mother encouraged me to be a court reporter . . . I became a lawyer (*Carla, 1986*)."

The Plush Pony dykes, however, always remained anonymous. Nameless, also, were the ways they overcame being underestimated. The intimacy in the portraits of butch lesbians in white A-shirts and baseball caps offers some entry into what their nightlives might have been like—that the Plush, as it was known to El Sereno locals, was where their gender nonconformity could be acknowledged and desired—but there's not a sense of articulated interiority nor a conversation between narrator and subject made as legible as the one in Latina Lesbians.

When I came to the Plush Pony, the bar signaled what it meant to be a brown, gender nonconforming queer from East Los Angeles—it was a time and space when one could traffic in the promiscuity between the aspirational lesbian and the rough queer. My queer adolescence took place at the convergence between the higher educational options that gave the subjects in Latina Lesbians language and empowerment, and the roughness of barrio nightlife captured in the deep creases of the subjects' faces in the Plush Pony series.

In 2001 I joined a softball team called Las Traviesas, which translates to "The Naughties." *Bueno, bonito, y barato* was our mantra. We were assembled by a mulleted East Los butch named Norma, who had recently broken up with the co-coach for the Redz, the last of the old-school lesbian haunts in Boyle Heights, and thus lost her coaching position.

I don't know who met Norma first, but our team was composed mostly of the Chicana lesbians I knew from the Thursday night weekly lesbian support group at one of the HIV prevention health service organizations near Beverly and Atlantic, where East Los turned into Montebello, where scrap met aspiration. We, too, were already losers. We had lost our posts as daughters in our families, lost jobs threatened by our legible queerness, and lost the barrio's respect for the choices we made regarding desire. We were *las tiradas,* the castaways, before we were Las Traviesas.

We talked sex, art, and policy, and ate vegetarian gorditas after lighting candles at the Virgin of Guadalupe altar in the parking lot at El Mercadito on Sundays, like good Chicana lesbians. For me, the time was at best an experiment in elusive authenticity and connecting with the likes of Norma and the posse she brought over with her from Redz, especially as I sought to imagine different models of female masculinity.

Much like the contextual specificities of each butch lesbian centered in the Plush Pony portraits, those representations were difficult to arrive at. My nascent Chicana lesbian spectatorship sought out visual registers to help name a difficult subjectivity within, one that wasn't ubiquitous in the early aughts when Google could bring queer worlds closer with just a few search terms. Back then, we had heard of Laura Aguilar because we were activists, but had never seen her work in the flesh. We had missed the few showings at the LGBT Center in West Hollywood or other presentations made possible by VIVA, a Latinx gay and lesbian advocacy group bringing awareness to the HIV/AIDS pandemic affecting Latinxs in Los Angeles County. VIVA was one of the few platforms for lesbian and gay Latinx artists to perform and show art where celebration and grief could coexist. We never saw Aguilar's work on the wall, but we had seen snapshots of her work in someone's photo album or on a flyer.

———

Even the most anonymous of Aguilar's subjects were more than phantom sightings at the dyke bar, situated at the end of a block in a predominantly working-class Latino neighborhood. They could have been Norma's friends in their early forties and equally enmeshed in the East Los lesbian bar scene. Vero, the catcher for Las Traviesas, was short, stocky, and had a carrot-colored bleach mop of hair styled after Norma's own mullet. She was even-keeled and always managed to calm Norma's bluster whenever the Redz team came up while they planned strategy. Man, Norma really had it out for the Redz.

The whole league seemed to have it out for Las Traviesas, a team untethered to a lesbian bar. A team composed of too many different kinds of Chicanas with different gradations of lesbian. A team with some of us in transit toward what we imagined to be queerer ports, queerer than what East Los Angeles was capable of making available to us at that time.

Our debut at Hazard Park was highly anticipated and the Redz was the first team we played. The innings flew past us. We were no batting match for the Redz's powerful pitcher, a copper-skinned badass with a ferocious windmill. Dalila—a talented shortstop whose comet-like throws never made contact with the butch on first base who couldn't catch for shit— was our only hope. The errors were stomach-turning for Norma. But they were fodder for the other teams. The Plush Pony old-timers were laughing at us, holding paper plates heavy with ceviche tostadas in one hand and gesturing wildly at the diamond with the other.

Halfway through the season, we were already in last place and I learned the other teams hated us and called us stuck-up. The dykes from other bars and teams thought we were too good for them because most of Las Traviesas had gone to college. They also thought most of us were attractive and catcalled some of our players by jersey numbers during games. None of us made any indication that we would date players from other teams, mostly because we were all partnered up. But also—we were stuck-up. We were stuck-up in the way institutions train you to be as you dust yourself off from barrio life and powder yourself in newer, better aspirations.

The season ended and Las Traviesas never made it out of last place. But it was a tithe to the community to allow us our proximity to *las duras*—to learn how to inhabit our skins and to heed caution when skin became a liability. Laura Aguilar never came to our games, nor was she privy to this particular tension playing out between the lesbians with names and the ones who went without. But East Los Angeles bar league lesbian softball allowed for a nuanced inhabiting of an experience that was alongside what Aguilar represented. In her own words from a 1988 artistic statement, Aguilar wanted "to provide a better understanding of what it's like to be a Latina and a Lesbian by showing images which allow us the opportunity to share ourselves openly, and to provide role models that break negative stereotypes and help develop a better bridge of understanding."

———

Aguilar's artistic corpus is only now circulating in institutional ways. The *Laura Aguilar: Show and Tell* retrospective traveled to Miami and opened at the Patricia & Phillip Frost Art Museum six weeks before Aguilar's death. Her 1993 photograph *Will Work For,* a self-portrait centering Aguilar holding a cardboard sign that reads "Artist Will Work For Axcess," in front of a building with the word GALLERY prominently displayed, reminds us twenty-five years later of the cultural precariat's means toward eking out a life. Aguilar endured as much danger alive as the opportunities her oeuvre will have in her death. Aguilar's prescient images brought to life the crumbling edges brown artists are compelled to navigate, the terrain she moved through as her name came to national and international platforms.

Aguilar's work has been continuously haunted by her own self-image as "ugly" and "fat," policing categories that demand those named to exist in lack. At the zenith of her career, Aguilar was able to break open and into a joy for her own brown abundance; an unabashed exploration that steers her outlaw body, a vessel among other vessels, toward generative and seditious destinations. Yet those of us who have lived in the prisons of wounding designations can attest that her work, especially the Grounded series of color photographs depicting Aguilar's body contracted and splayed in gestures that mirror the earthen spheroid formations in Joshua Tree National Park, is both respite and revolution in its wild hinterland of quiet intensity.

———

I am attesting as someone who has, too, lived in the prison of wounding—a wounding unto my own body and a wounding onto my most beloved others and their desires to love my wounded body—to know that letting my own body splay over the soft rocks of Hidden Valley, Split Rock Loop Trail, Arch Rock, and Indian Cove Boy Scout Trail is an act of setting myself free. To walk unencumbered by the trapping of modernity through the shadows of Mojave yucca plants, ocotillos, and gravel trails—to piss in the wind and jerk off into the shadowy parts of the canyons—means that I can be as free as those who own the land on which I stand and make my own land art. I've stood in one place, in several places over the years, for hours just to see the light change over the landscape. It might be prayer. It might be what grounds me to surrender to the ancestral seizures that make themselves known to me.

Waiting for more moths to alight from my lazy pompadour—is that you, Big Poppa? Showing me the way to the light?

Or how I might get over the breakup that broke me down for the last time on the side of the road near the Cottonwood Springs entrance of a national park. These are the ways I come to recalibrate how I see the vastness of my own body held in the center of Joshua Tree's vastness.

For Laura, whose body took up much of the air and space of any given social configuration she inhabited, I imagine that her coming to the desert meant making and taking an opportunity to be small. What might it mean to revel in the aura of smallness? To forget the bulldagger-in-a-china-shop policing of self for a moment and take in the safety offered in the eternity of sky above. In a city, in a dark, red-bulbed dancehall, a smoky bar in the bottoms of El Sereno, the large bodies of gender renegades are read as suspect in both appetite and desire. Good lays, bad citizens. Laura takes those suspicions and distills them in the photographs of her body, where she captures herself in the middle. She cropped many of the images to make her body appear as another presumed object taking its rightful place in the natural environment—another boulder, another mass of sediment containing the narrative of collision where two, three, or unknown numbers of cultures come to situate in the folds of her rippling belly or the stretch marks on her back. The largesse of that gesture seems only right to settle into a space like Joshua Tree, haven for the thing it's named after, and haven for embodied sites of excess, and weary in the face of inevitable extinction.

———

Early Spanish explorers and settlers perceived Joshua Tree as a wasteland. In the 1850s, Mormon pioneers encountered the species of desert flora and named it after Joshua, who raised his hands to the sky in prayer, according to the Biblical story, a discursive mirror for the Joshua tree's long prickly branches raised skyward. In the late 1800s, miners and early homesteaders made attempts to settle the land, leaving behind evidence of those efforts with the Lost Horse and Desert Queen

Mines, and the Desert Queen Ranch. It wasn't until the early twentieth century that South Pasadena socialite and amateur gardener Minerva Hoyt made Joshua Tree trendy. Hoyt lobbied for more than twenty years to create a protected desert park where she could quiet the internal noise and find renewed health in the clean air, as well as beauty in its unrelenting topography. The name Joshua Tree National Monument was chosen to honor the park's most unique inhabitant.

In Aguilar's Grounded series, shot in 2006 and 2007, there's an elemental allusion to being earthbound. As a queer brown butch, I can't help but make my own affective assignations to the longing in the photographs of Aguilar in Joshua Tree, the ways her body sits, back to the camera as if in some heartbroken repose, the landscape embracing what's left of her body in wait and in the quietest of want. What the body wants is the earthliest of desires and in Aguilar's bodily charge the desire is as immense as the rock formations it mirrors. In the interstitial space where my identity lives alongside my own desire to scrutinize, I wander on to Aguilar with eyes closed, her naked belly spilling over into the narcissistic mirrors on the surfaces of puddles that dot the New Mexican landscape in the *Nature Self-Portrait* series (1996) as if to plead to a lover or a swath of land, *Will you ever be mine?*

Following her recent death, however, it's hard for me not to think of the ways the earthly qualities of Aguilar's portraits—of desire situated in a land left in its own wild repose—refract the hauntological nature of brown bodies traveling through the west or, in this particular juncture, Joshua Tree. Joshua Tree is often cast as a site for Pinterest-plucked fantasies of pioneering hipsters heading into the high desert to escape the demands of urban modernity and capitalist fatalism. But in Aguilar's hands Joshua Tree remains a site haunted by the lost excesses of brown queer desire. In Aguilar's hands, we remember that Joshua Tree as a national park is a place just as available to the blue-collar butches holding court over the pool tables of the Plush Pony as it is to the tech industry's nouveau riche lesbian programmers, who prove to the dominant culture that queers can contribute to the gross national product too. And while I may remember Joshua Tree as the setting for an older and possibly wiser Laura Aguilar as the vulnerable sad butch splayed on the rocks for queer and brown publics to behold and to continue beholding even more closely in her death, I am reminded of another specter of working-class beauty and grace—the living ghost of Tejana pop queen Selena, a patron saint of joyful femme ebullience dancing in the foreground of another Joshua Tree. Selena holds a particular type of hold over the desert in the video for "Amor Prohibido," filmed in Joshua Tree thirteen years before Aguilar created her own California desert oeuvre. Her Tejana femme vulnerability is situated in a classed conflict that, on first listen to the song, suggests a parallel to warring families a la Capulets and Montagues intervening in young love. But on closer examination there's an economic quandary: that despite being poor, everything the speaker of the song gives is better than money. Both Selena and Aguilar not only ignite Joshua Tree with the particular travails of a heart in want, but they also offer a response to the majesty of its grandeur through gesture and image that pollinate its landscape with indelible histories that speak to the quotidian manifestations of the border wound. Their presence invites me to consider how the colonial encounter and the ways in which the u.s.–Mexican War and the Mexican Revolution—losing the collectivism of the ejído system to the profit-maximizing hacienda system, for example—persist in everyday relationships that brown queers try to enact with each other and with the land in various points along the Southwest. Selena and Aguilar, respectively, speak of a love that is forbidden, and so why not enact that queer contraband in the lost trails of this barren hinterland? A prohibition of desire that pulsates all the more ecstatically among the trees Mormons named Joshua in the ascetic setting of the California high desert.

And thus, a dance emerges between star-crossed lovers of mixed economic backgrounds and blood—the butch lawyers and the femme sex workers of Aguilar's portraitures, the girl on the wrong side of the "Amor Prohibido" railroad tracks. This dance emerges and flirts with recognition and visibility, leaving the penumbra of anonymity in its wake. It gets choreographed between an austere landscape like Joshua Tree and its partner in brown excess; to see the movement of every wrinkle like it were desert mallow, every keloid like churro cholla, every bit of broken skin blooming in liberated relief. Laura Aguilar and Selena have both trafficked in those excessive intersections through a radical praxis of their brownness. This is a malleable brownness that sits and lays corpulently in the annals of art and popular culture, misperceived and misaligned as well as in the valleys of Joshua Tree, a mestizaje of suspicion where two bodies in a desert sing in similar and simultaneous registers of scarcity and plethora.

Memories of the Skin:
Shizu Saldamando's Portraits

2018 | One April weekend, as I saw the first sign for East Los Angeles herald my homecoming, I decided to text the artist Shizu Saldamando. She lived near the Atlantic exit where I pulled off the 60 Freeway to pump gas at Southern California prices, a jolt from what I had been paying in Tucson. I was bound for a wedding in San Diego and needed a gift for the bride, an aging punk with a penchant for revolutionary histories, like any one of us who came of age going to Los Crudos shows at Macondo or seeing Jawbreaker at Jabberjaw in the nineties. Shizu's studio was an ideal alternative to the tyranny of wedding registries. I arrived, parked my car in the densely packed residential street, and met Shizu in her driveway. We hugged hello and sauntered over to the brightly lit home studio in her and her husband Len's backyard. I was ready to pick out one of Shizu's paño prints, images rendered in ballpoint blue ink on handkerchiefs, a style inspired by jailhouse pinta art out of the Southwest. The paño I chose was a portrait of Alice Bag, which seemed appropriate to fulfill the "something blue" mandate for rebellious brides who know the words to "Babylonian Gorgon."

As I handled the handkerchief delicately, I looked around the studio and saw a new series of works on paper and pine wood canvases in various beginning stages. While the work was new, the subjects in each individual portrait were familiar to me. There was the queer club promoter, the punk singer, the ranchera goth chanteuse—subjects off the canvas who I've known for the last two decades as we try to make centers out of margins, hashtags out of undergrounds. Or mostly arguing and finally relenting on Morrissey's relevance. They were just a few of the reasons I was excited to be back in my familiar East Los, watching the downtown city skyline silhouette against a smog-streaked sunset in the rearview mirror of my 4Runner.

———————

My parents found each other one Valentine's Day evening on the third floor of El Mercadito, the last standing identifiable grand central market located on East 1st Street and Lorena. My upbringing was one in which every kid I encountered— from kindergarten to junior high—had a parent that came to the United States from some other far-flung place in the world. We were the majority in southeast Los Angeles and no one felt like their outsiderness outdid anyone else's. We were all translating utility bills to our parents, asking permission to join the Brownies or to try out for our little Catholic school's talent show. We sold the world's finest chocolates to get to Knott's Berry Farm. Our heroes were James Worthy and Fernando Valenzuela. We were lucky to grow up in a time and place where our heroes looked like us.

Seeing ourselves on our terms was always important, and Shizu gets that. In my years as a chronicler of Los Angeles-based artists of color, and their practices, creative ethos, and cultural contributions, I've known homegrown talents like Rudy (Bleu) Garcia, Martín Sorrondeguy (Singer of Los Crudos and Limp Wrist), and Lizette Gutierrez (known as San Cha) as important members of a brown commons, a potentially radical space that, according to the late queer theorist José Muñoz, would be inhabited by both working-class Latinx queer immigrants and queer punks and artists of color in service to a collective good. Subjects whose queerness becomes saturated with colors and sparkle that heighten the complicated gradations of self. Shizu has always had the ability to home in on her subjects' individual modes of resistance. These modes—a faraway look, a defiant smirk, a swirling sea of baby-blue tulle—push against the dominant white heterosexual culture that stratifies much of a Los Angeles to which these subjects find themselves adjacent and sometimes in opposition.

Shizu was gearing up for a new solo exhibition in June at the Charlie James Gallery in Chinatown. This was her first solo work since her survey exhibition at the Vincent Price Art Museum (VPAM), located on the East Los Angeles College campus, in the fall of 2008. Back then Shizu was still single and living in West Los Angeles, off Sawtelle, in a cramped second-floor apartment above the one where her Japanese grandmother lived until her death a few years later. It was also her workspace and I remember having to wash my eyes out with cold water thanks to the chemicals she was working with in the small kitchen.

The ethos that lives east of the river has come out unabashedly in Shizu's new work. And coming out is important.

At the heart of this new series, called *To Return,* are Shizu's reflections on her own current sociability as an east-of-the-river denizen, which any self-respecting Angeleno knows is where the true Eastside begins and ends. Every first Friday of the month, Len takes care of their toddler while Shizu heads to Chico's to catch a bevy of nascent performance artists cutting their teeth on the dance floor of Club Scum, the monthly dance party that centers queer brown members of an ever-growing identity spectrum, where new names for self emerge and tumble out like fractals from a disco ball. Shizu is now part of an East Los Angeles marked by histories of radical affinities between Chicanx activists decrying the casualty inequities in the Vietnam War. An East Los Angeles that was home to young queers navigating homophobia in their own homes as well as racism in West Hollywood, Los Angeles's perceived center of LGBT acceptance. In between those two poles, the cultural shifting took place through a political agitation that Shizu has always been adjacent to. That proximity has compelled her to contemplate her own vexed gender role, especially as her world has become peopled by queer and trans people in East L.A.

"Five years ago I was still having an extended adolescence. I went out and partied and I still do," Shizu tells me recently, a few days before her show opens at Charlie James. "But now that I'm married and in a positive, supportive partnership, I have a kid, all of that has allowed me to free a lot of internalized misogyny, this baggage that I didn't know I carried as far as what it means to have a voice."

The moment we're in is new. This is a moment with a real chance at becoming a movement that might just benefit everyone who isn't a Hollywood, A-list, white actress. A movement that goes beyond social media and into disrupting norms and mores that produce toxic gender performances. And right now, nothing crystalizes that possibility more than what the #MeToo movement has allowed us to witness. And question.

Does having seen Harvey Weinstein do a perp walk allow all of us assigned female at birth to retreat into ourselves and take inventory of the varying degrees of trauma we carry? And how do our most beloved L.A. artists arrive at such reckonings?

"Before I wondered: how does a single woman communicate, have her own voice and still be attractive to whoever she wants?" Shizu says before her smartphone short circuits and the call is dropped. "I look back, realize there was all this formative gender performing that that we do. You wake up and realize you were raised a certain way and then you get to the point where you're just like, 'I don't care.'"

————

I had last seen Shizu back in early December 2017 at Chico's in Montebello. We had been invited to celebrate our friend Martín Sorrondeguy's fiftieth birthday bash, a cinquentañera he called it, with queer tongue firmly in cheek. I wasn't surprised to see Shizu still snapping photographs on her banged-up, nearly obsolete digital camera, a relic hanging off her tattooed wrist, clinking between our vodka sodas. Some shots she snaps are gold. Others, like a photo of me with artist Joey Terrell, show up blurry the next day.

We had seen Martín wail and stomp for Limp Wrist numerous times at The Smell in downtown L.A., as well as hold our centers of gravity in mosh pits for Murder City Devils, and we'd even played it cool meeting TV on the Radio's Tunde Adebimpe and his bubbly Nigerian mother at the Trader Joe's in Silver Lake the day before Thanksgiving one year. Catching up at Chico's after fifteen years of friendship meant being able to catch sight of Martín making a big birthday entrance in black leather suspenders and a buoyant, baby-blue tulle ballerina skirt, bobbing curtsies to every one of his nearing admirers.

A cornerstone of Shizu's work is making visible the youth cultures she has been a part of for the last twenty years in such a way that expresses an ontology of the ordinary; a soft whisper that reveals enough without revealing the secrets of these complicated public identities and the scary abysses within very private selves. Why do we like the music we do? Or dress the way we do? Why do we still feel weird enough to hold up the walls at most parties or rock shows? How do those questions feed into a competing matrix of desire? Her photographs capture some essence of each person and become a blueprint in which she carefully isolates the contexts of her subjects—to remove the inaudibility that comes when the bass is bouncing or when a fight is breaking out on the dance floor.

However, Shizu is stretching beyond the isolating impulse and allowing for some play in her work. This shift can be most notably experienced in the piece from that party at Chico's, now hanging at Charlie James, titled *Martin's Cinquentañera*. Shizu's portrayal of the blue tulle as swirling wave suggests a queer metaphysical take on the image of the goddess Yemaya, a Venus-like deity known as the mother of the ocean in a religion called Santería in parts of the Caribbean, Florida, and the Southwest; Candomblé in Brazil; and Yoruba in Nigeria. A reassuring figure who protects her children, Yemaya is ultimately a beacon of solace for her believers. The sight of Martín's sexy defiance can offer a similarly important spiritual shelter for queer children of all ages seeking recognition and belonging in one of the most antagonistic times for, especially, queer and trans youth fighting to stay with families being torn apart by ICE. In a visual language made raw by queer punk rock parlance, it's not hard to imbue Martín's unapologetic selfhood, in his tough and flamboyant stance and direct gaze back out to the spectator, with an aura of knowing protectiveness, one animated by the fact that only twenty years ago not all gay man of color were guaranteed a chance to enter middle age on their own terms.

For Shizu, it is important to be in service by making those images possible, not just as an ally to and for the community by whom she feels most comprehended, but also as an accomplice. Activating an ally position means aiding and abetting a queerness that makes queer spaces like Chico's, a bar that's been in her neighborhood since the late nineties and is her preferred partying zone, part and parcel to Shizu's cultural contributions. But how does that fly for members of a queer community whose spatial options, including housing, are diminishing with each new threat of gentrification? Is there a tendency to barricade against a hostile hetero world, including its hetero defectors? Is Shizu like those straight women in the third season of *Crazy Ex-Girlfriend,* episode nine, where White Josh brings his straight brofriend to Home Base, the local gay bar, only to be inundated by revelers from a bachelorette party gone awry? Straight women go to gay bars for a reason, and the promise of safety to let it all hang out sometimes outweighs the gay misogyny—as evidenced in White Josh's disapproving grimace—confirming that the women's presence is not welcome. And sometimes gay misogyny is easier to absorb; it's the energy of a verbal joust rather than the physically menacing misogyny connected to hetero masculinity. Both are toxic, but if the *Handmaid's Tale* is any indication of how hetero femininity is feeling these days, then one devil might be better than the other.

It might be time to take up new mantles.

"I've always depicted a lot of queer people in my work just because that's who's always been in my weird, musical underground. There's a certain level of comfort in seeing an acceptance of fluidity in these spaces, our spaces, that a lot of other communities don't have," Shizu tells me over a Skype chat.

"You mean, like, straight spaces," I query, hearing my voice crack on the word *straight*.

"There's a level of intelligence I value because it's not just a level of safety but just a more intellectually gratifying [sociability]," Shizu answers. "I'm challenged more as someone who is queer adjacent to think about my own subjectivity as well."

For longtime Club Scum promoter and producer Rudy Garcia, who goes by his nom de party Rudy Bleu, Shizu's work is reflective of a culture and scene that he has inhabited his whole life. She has been an active participant in the scene for more than a decade. People appreciate the courtesy Shizu demonstrates in asking to take a photograph at a party—her transparency is important to Rudy, who says she is not producing exploitative portraiture but documenting a time and a space that is important to her community.

"Shizu captures the energy of this scene," Rudy says to me in a voice message sent over Facebook. "Seeing myself and my friends in art on art walls is that same feeling I got seeing Joey Terrell's work for the first time. I was seeing queer Chicanos in an art setting, which meant finally getting to see myself."

Shizu's artistic process becomes visible when she deejays Club Scum parties, providing a service to a community in need of conviviality, to hold another on a dance floor that allows for both love and grief to coexist each week. Taking in and putting out—a symbiosis of labor that allows for Shizu to contribute to both a queer everyday life in which her subjects' images circulate, and an everynight life to boot. She understands the crowd there, revels in having the same musical tastes, and trusts that her own tastes provide some semblance of aural pleasure for the dancers.

———

The depths of hanging out as an aging participant of the underground are contingent on that underground providing ample opportunities for a continuing education. A dance floor should be a site of ontological meditation, a four-four beat reminding you that there's only now. Of Frida Kahlo's inimitable portraiture, the essayist John Berger noted that the Mexican artist could signal that "there was no future, only an immensely modest present which claimed everything and to which the things painted momentarily return whilst we look, things which were already memories before they were painted, memories of the skin." Or in other words, the moment—like the moment captured in the portrait *Vicki and Audrey, Chicas Rockeras,* with two punk rock millennials in the middle of mentoring pre-teen punks rock camp–style in Huntington Park, a barrio of Southeast Los Angeles—is not the past but a muscular presence redefined with each spectatorial visitation. How does Berger's idea of modest presence interact with or even counteract José Muñoz's theory of queer futurity, which posits that our queerness has not yet arrived? How might this presence feel its way through the dark in the world that Shizu has devoted her life to making? How does an allyship that verges on radical accomplice-hood serve to bridge the two where an artist can render queer memory on a skin made complicated through its occupation of desire and aspiration?

"Wait, are you going by 'they' now?" Shizu asks me recently over a Fourth of July lunch at a Cuban eatery in Downey, where my parents live and where I'm staying for much of the summer. Our server has more than a passing resemblance to Juan Gabriel, who Shizu refers to as goth, the Mexican pop icon who passed away suddenly two years ago.

"I actually like other peoples' preferred gender pronouns for me. It's more fun than choosing one myself," I retort. "I get to see where people are at with their perceptions." We share the fried plantains and clink our white wine glasses like the punk godparents we have become.

A few days later I receive a text from Shizu asking me to moderate a panel of emerging artists whose work is being exhibited in the gallery downstairs from her show at Charlie James. The original moderator, Guadalupe Rosales, the digital archivist behind Instagram sensation *Veteranas & Rucas,* has fallen ill from a bee sting. I arrive early on the second hottest day of the summer, clocking in at 103 degrees. Tucson has prepared me well for such heat, but then most places in Los Angeles aren't equipped with central air. The lot of us inside the gallery space are miserable but hiding it well.

Shizu introduces the artists, and everyone in the room is adhering to some variation of gender nonconformity. I ask about the chronicling of underground publics, but we talk about process and Instagram. Floral print and goth tank tops are ubiquitous, as is La Croix. Many of Shizu's recent subjects are in the room.

"[Shizu] captures authentic moments, the personalities of peoples whose pictures she takes and transforms into sketches without being invasive," says Audrey Silvestre, a UCLA doctoral student, whose face along with her girlfriend's hang on the walls of the gallery. "Her presence doesn't change the vibe, whether at punk spaces or queer spaces. It's weird to think of her as an outsider."

Do I Love San Anto?

2019 | This excursion into another southwest horizon wouldn't be complete without a Texas reverie. I was in a rental car, the window open, taking in the afternoon breeze outside San Antonio in late March, three interminable years into the Trump presidency. It was the start of a queer weekend and it felt like spring, which in Texas means a humidity. The kind of humid jolt that makes your hair bloom and skin glisten as it sneaks up on you in this part of the Lone Star State.

It had been a while since I found myself inside a car gridlocked by a slowly moving parking lot, inching forward a mile or two at a time. I was in the butt of a joke about Los Angeles made strange by the huge Texas flag waving in slow motion on the passenger side. It marked my welcome to San Antonio, a city that has always had a fraught meaning to my Angeleno nationalist, Californian, ambiguously brown self. *Chicana* and *Chicanx* still had much to prove to me as appropriate vessels for my failing identitarian loyalties. But the city of the Alamo provoked my contrarian desires for belonging to an identity forged in struggle. Here in Military City, USA, the patriotism bounces off the walls. San Antonio's home to four military installations and is known as the mother-in-law of the Army.

Soldiers and cadets in the military have been matchmade with local bachelorettes and debutantes. Heterosexuality might be the thing that is bigger than Texas.

On the other side of contradiction highway, San Antonio offers me several wonderful experiences in Texas-style icehouse slash gay clubs, all clustered conveniently together across the street from Luther's all-night diner. The Fruit Loop, as it was known to me in the haze of a drunken hour and typically over a plate of smothered homefries, touts the best karaoke, the best two-step, and the best Selena-at-the-Astrodome drag queen impersonators, all within range of each other. The San Antonio poet and my friend Joe Jiménez was often my sole karaoke audience, singing along to my drunken rendition of Marco Antonio Solís's "Si No Te Hubieras Ido."

The spectacles seem to top one another as you move, again drunkenly, through the caverns that connect these places, much like a funhouse. And there are never enough dykes in this hall of mirrors. There are plenty of lesbians, coupled off with strict barriers. Probably military, too. But there is no cavorting openly outside of established social groups—endemic for those who are newly out. I wasn't newly anything and the clubs were rainbow adherent, had probably doubled their prices during Pride season, but I was a visitor who would always leave. The queer relations here felt burdened by constraints of the political imagination, as if our similar identity markers automatically meant a shared politic. I was always aware of the proximities and distances that other queer and brown identity politicians had to Mexicanidad and the means to which whiteness always managed to be re-centered without the utterance of direct language, just oblique suggestions.

During one of my previous visits to San Antonio, I was with Cornerstone Theater Company, a cross-cultural collaborative ensemble project founded by Bill Rauch thirty-five years ago. I had come to interview Tejanos impacted by and living with HIV and AIDS. I led story circles and wrote short plays based on the dialogues culled from those meetings with everyday people—older gay men, former drug addicts, and those who were infected in the eighties through blood infusions. We were a crew of six from Los Angeles—myself and two gay men, one Latino, plus our tech and actors—and we returned several times to stage a performance where real people and actors shared monologues for a hometown audience at the historic Teatro Guadalupe, which operated as the "most opulent" movie theater from 1942 until it fell into disrepair and was closed in 1970. The city had rehabbed the theater in 1984, making it an ideal cultural center for the traditional Mexican community of the West Side. Today it is part of the larger Guadalupe Cultural Arts Center, which continues to program culturally relevant projects and art events. I remember being wowed by the vintage art deco floors, feeling the warmth of its turbulent history in the bones of the building. I remember falling in love with every single community member who stepped out for the first time to talk about their hopes and fears around living with HIV.

But the theater experience was another strange encounter with the city, facilitated by Gilead, the pharmaceutical company that hired Cornerstone to do the story circles and to stage public readings. In hindsight, I can't believe I participated in making art on Big Pharma's dime to help people feel okay about starting treatment. But Cornerstone is where I got my nonprofit paycheck and PPO coverage. They paid for my flight and hotel. I had a per diem. Everything else was impoverishing. Why would my imagination be spared?

Do I love San Anto?

I like the buying power my California dollars have had here. It has gotten me into the casual trouble that a brown big city queer dyke with arrested development typically encounters. But I was from Los Angeles, the lesser metropole with a messier cost of living. The one most people like to dump on until they come to visit, fall in love with neighborhoods previously inhabited by my friends' Latino immigrant parents, and see that it's not just *Baywatch*. Sports people were one sector that consistently bagged on L.A. One time I was at a late afternoon beer bust during a stressful game between the Lakers and the Spurs, and the dyke bar had a huge screen, ceiling to floor. I stood in front of it and *whoa'ed* when Shaq did something impressive with a pass. A dunk? Was I already blitzed by that point? One of the locals wearing Spurs everything asked me, in that way where you don't hear the question mark at the end of the sentence, if I was a Lakers fan. *Oh . . . no, not at all.* I was teetering in nervous judgment but I still knew my place. I bought a round instead.

I nurtured my alcoholic tendencies and soothed my insecurities this way—at the gay bars on Main Avenue while cruising only for friendship and temporary nonsexual intimacies with strangers in similar straits. Bought more rounds that totaled to eleven dollars at Bar America, its orange faux leather seats as bright as the scenes from the John Sayles's film *Lone Star,* which still play to this day in the movie theater of my third eye. My dollars went all night here, it's true. I didn't have the sticker shock of West Hollywood's double-digit well drinks or price of gas or butchphobia to worry me.

I always came back and art was always the occasion— whether it was a two-week residency with my old performance art collective, Butchlalis de Panochtitlan, at the long-running Jump-Start Performance Company in the King William Historic

District, or the music and museum industry conferences that I attended in the past lives of my twenties and thirties. The conferences were always held in and around the city's famed Riverwalk, and each time I demurred successfully from seeing the Alamo with my colleagues.

San Antonio is excessive. It brings out the sugar hound in me. I think of the pan dulce display at Mi Rancho. I think of the portions. I think of neon pink prickly pear cocktails. I think of my father's weeping wound on his arm from the diabetes he fails to Master Cleanse. I remember my bootleg Frida Kahlo Converse high-top sneakers at the penultimate day of one Fiesta San Antonio celebration, a yearly, ten-day-long event and one of the biggest moneymakers for the city, which has overseen it for well over a century. Fiesta is a street party that seems divorced now from its original purpose—to commemorate the Battle of Flowers, a parade that celebrated the liberation of Texas from Mexico in the Battles at the Alamo in the winter of 1835 and San Jacinto in the spring of 1836. Divorced in the sense that the whole thing is peopled by Mexico's descendants cavorting to the Tejano rhythms of Ram Herrera and feeling the boozy sugar rush from the individual-sized pitchers of daiquiri or margarita. It's the way these historical losses inspire deep-fried Dionysian binges that satiate one or all senses that feels familiar to me.

I saw my friend, the poet Joe Jiménez, as I slowly drove along the downtown street to where my GPS was leading me. Seeing Joe right off the bat was the queer omen I needed. I had on a lightweight bomber jacket, but he wore a classic weight-lifting tank top, and rightfully so, for he was a rippled muscle majesty. Joe's poetry is much like his appearance—pure masculine beauty in a panoramic state of longing. We had met twenty years earlier in Los Angeles, when I lived with a mutual friend of his who threw a party for Joe at a café in Hollywood called Espresso Mi Cultura, during which Joe gave a reading that stunned us baby brown queers into silence. I stopped and coasted along the sidewalk near to where he stood and wolf-whistled as I rolled down the passenger window. *My favorite San Anto joto,* I swooned. Joe smiled shyly and waved me off to primo parking.

I was excited to see rafa's new work, in the simultaneous familiarity and cultural estrangement that Texas provided. I hadn't seen him since January of that year when he debuted a performance at a large-scale event I co-hosted called Variedades. Rafa's body had been "airbrushed," painted into a bright Mexican Rose and styled into an embodied lowrider. That's right—rafa made his body a site of dropped and faded glory, complete with East Los Angeles underground performance artist, Cyclona, painted over the entirety of his backside. Rafa dropped to his knees on an imagined catwalk and turned his head in profile to a roaring crowd. He struck poses, wearing stunning gold-plated jewelry braided into his ponytail and salon-styled mani-cured gels, the tips curling into glorious swoops, encrusted with colorful zirconias. Fucking legendary. The protective older sibling in me hoped this city had rolled out the red carpet for his talent.

As I walked away from my parked car, I wondered if this place, which looked like all the other places that call them-selves contemporary art centers, would be different. It's not a museum—a museum has a permanent collection that draws on and reflects particular histories while also keeping the bene-ficiaries of those histories at arm's length. I would learn a few nights later at the annual fundraising banquet that the contem-porary art center was named ArtPace, after the owner Linda Pace, who was a locally beloved arts patron and daughter of

David Earl Pace of Pace Foods. *Pace Foods? Like Pace Picante? The gringo salsa Get-a-rope-Pace-Picante?* Yes, the very one.

The space itself was like many contemporary arts centers I have been to, and much like the contemporary arts center I had worked at just a few years prior—big, boxy, bright, and existing in the monochromatic schemas of whites, beiges, blacks, and grays. On the off days, my old workplace also served as the site where the late Steve Jobs would reveal the latest tech gadget to the masses. That workplace would slowly but surely devote itself to tech companies needing venues to court venture capital firms or hold luncheons for CEOS to bloviate over women in tech. Bless the art workers in their unfettered desire to create space for art and those with ambiguous relationships to creative endeavors. I am conscious of these places in a way that living under capitalism requires me to be—living with an unexamined gratitude for places where artists can ascend to greater visibility, for curators who bring in artists from marginalized communities. However, the gallery is always a business. That and the tempered rage that is the 501c3 model and the healthcare insurance it's tethered to are the best we can do for the workers who facilitate those organized spectacles. It's often a difficult way to build a livelihood unless you, like Linda Pace, come from generational wealth.

Again, I was met with the familiarity with the bright jewel-toned accent walls in the lobby, in line with the upscale *rasquache* often utilized to satisfy tourists' expectations of these downtown Southwest locales. I saw in the periphery of my vision the persistent recognition of a copper-toned signature in soil, dry and blanketing the ground under our feet, making the strangeness of the antiseptic gallery space more welcoming to those of us in Tejanas, Stetsons, Ropers, and tennis shoes. I felt the thrill running through my body, that familiar feeling that comes with seeing my friend's ideas about matrilineal beauty, labor, history, and spectacle spilling into public spaces and washing over me. And I wanted, of course, to delay the gratification by looking away.

The food trucks out front signaled the masses who had gathered around tacos and beer. I scanned the grounds, taking in the hetero to homo ratio packed into the space of ArtPace as I marched toward the wine and snagged a small plastic cup of Chardonnay. I wondered if I would spot Joe, hoping for some queer alliance against the displays of varied hetero configurations. There were young families out alongside older couples, all of them Tejano, all of them scoring high on my compulsory heterosexuality exams. I was suddenly conscious of my solitude, aware that I had no one with whom to negotiate my time or space, nor to check in with at home. I scanned the hometown team on the patio again. Would they glean the queer contents in the gallery space? And if so, would they care? And if not, did it matter? They had as much a right to the conviviality the evening offered as anyone else, and the queer expressions I felt protective over could be the healing elixir that might allow for my sense of belonging to deepen here. I took a deep breath to calm or summon my nervous system before heading inside again.

I stopped right at the lip of the entrance to *With Land*, the title of rafa's exhibit. It was full of people and I knew I would come back the next day to take in the show again when the gallery emptied and quieted down. But in that moment we all stood on the adobe fundament of a prolonged intimate creation, the fruit of labor salted by rafa's sweat, the turn of his hands through earth soil, horse dung, bales of hay, and water— and lots of it, as it blanketed the entirety of the floors in the central gallery and touched every part of the four walls. I had been to several of rafa's adobe-based projects, each one touched by the hands of his inner circles and close collaborators in Marfa and Los Angeles. But tonight I could sense the loneliness in the space of his work. The entirety of adobe bricks, panels, sculptures, and floor space were his and now he gifted them to us, a temple in disguise. We, the followers and zealots.

It was a familiar material in various forms, activated with our bodies and sentience and our willingness for prolonged engagement with the histories these objects before us hoped to conjure. There were new bricks laid in ritualistic configurations, gestures to pyramids we could imagine with the help of the Xoloitzcuintli dog figures in protective repose at their feet. Rafa had also fashioned the adobe material into large panels that hung on the wall like empty portraits. You'd pivot your neck until your gaze quickly fell upon one panel in which he had painted a stunning portrait of his maternal grandmother, Doña Guadalupe, a stately and serious Indigenous woman from a small township called Ricardo Flores Magón in the Northern Mexico state of Durango. Doña Guadalupe's presence loomed large enough to convince me at times that all five feet and eight inches of her were truly with us. Rafa had worked on this show for a few weeks prior to the exhibition's opening that night and was staying in the loft apartment a few floors up from the galleries.

I ran into a local university professor who was a big fan of rafa's work. She was a cultural studies scholar who seemed to me more like a gushing fan with a big research fund that allowed her to fly to Los Angeles, New York, Mexico City, or Tucson at a moment's notice to see her favorite artists. I envied her resources but didn't have it in me to sustain the institutional damage on my psyche, seeing what it has done to friends and foes alike. I stared at the scholar's receding hairline and the broken capillaries on her cheeks and smiled politely at her halitosis as she recounted the latest drama in her department. *This couldn't be me.* But, also, I really didn't consider what weight my MFA would grant me in the world of academia. I only went back to grad school to escape the soft authoritarian hamster wheel of my last nine-to-five and to live in a more economically viable city for my persistent underemployment, continuing displacement cycles in the desert town where I could afford to live alone. Oh, and there was the possibility of getting my ex back while I was at it. Being alive was expensive and academia was hardly worse than a full-time job in its subtle insidiousness for disciplining the errant subject. Holding on to errancy meant holding on to my rasquachismo. And I was incapable of opting for stability through civility. I wasn't mad; I just lacked that constitution, that refinement. Instead I counted on them, as did most of my artist friends in-between projects, for paid gigs every other year. The beauty of quarters and semesters meant new blood, holding at bay old age and the constant specter of precarity as long as Wall Street didn't tank any more university endowments for the foreseeable future. I still appreciate academics helping artists delay poverty, by the hour.

The scholar went on about the spring break that never was and I caught sight of the first of my Angeleñxs in town, decked out in their finest borderlands runway looks. Sebastian Hernández, clad in everything black leather—vest, pants, and boots—and serving daddy vaquero looks on the somber soil runway.

Sebastian was blindfolded but still more sure-footed than many of us in the room. They moved forward and backward, arms stretched out toward willing participants, tinfoil-wrapped numbers and letters lodged into different sides of their Stetson brims, glinting, quivering as they moved, catching the light of a setting sun. Sebastian made contact with a long and loose-haired, scraggly bearded young man and they hugged in the middle of the space and swayed a bit, side to side, to an imaginary music only they could hear. But they were mostly holding each other still. It was a prolonged embrace between two young, masculine-presenting beings on display, yet the length of time marked the intimacy between them. They stopped being strangers or were only strange to themselves.

Mid-way through the performance, in between the adobe Xoloitzcuintli dogs set in tableau throughout the gallery, Sebastian suddenly let go of the young, bearded man and began to move carefully toward their next partner. Sebastian found at their side a woman in a black cotton dress with a red, plaid, long-sleeved shirt. Sebastian carefully and slowly moved their fingertips along her hand and arm until their hand made it to the top of her shoulder. They brought their other hand to her other shoulder and Sebastian moved in for a hug. The woman received them and wrapped her arms around Sebastian's lithe body. They smiled at each other, the body language relaxed and genuinely warm as if they knew one another already. And they did, as I found out shortly thereafter; the woman was the curator of the exhibition, Risa Puleo. Once she and Sebastian parted, the blindfold came off and the Bic lighter appeared. Sebastian took off the Stetson—a sign of tried-and-true Texan prosperity—and I got a clearer view of what the tin-wrapped words spelled out: WILD DESIRE. And the numbers were a year: 1836. Since we were gathered in San Antonio, I assumed the reference had to do with the city's largest historical wound, and a quick Google search confirmed that 1836 was the year of the Battle of the Alamo. The year that is implied in the call to arms *Remember the Alamo*. What they mean is to remember the several hundred Texans who lost their bid for freedom from Mexico's army, led by General Santa Anna, after a nearly two-week-long siege at the Alamo mission. Back when this was Mexican Texas.

The silence was crackling with electricity as the audience quietly watched Sebastian light their cowboy crown on fire. A baby cooing in the background caught my ear's attention, a reminder that the room was a spectrum of disclosures and disavowals of brownness and the various vectors of identification. There were those who knew themselves completely and those who questioned their compulsory assignments inherited from family, tradition, or the state. And there were those who might not see Sebastian outside of their masculine drag. WILD DESIRE went up in flames. An awareness of these identities, of course, comes laden with all kinds of assumptions and expectations embodied within our proximities and distances to a Mexico that exposes the many myths that move through us and through the corners of our Latinidad problem. And Sebastian knows that. Whether it's the unexamined privileges of mestizaje and the white supremacy subtly cloaked in our language and relationality, or the toxic worship of Virgin of Guadalupe statues and our consent to maintaining the erasures of Indigenous thought and practice, Sebastian has a way of calling these colonized histories to account.

The hat burned into a smoldering mess, quickly put out with one stomp of Sebastian's boot. I remembered that Sebastian's last object of desire was a hunky, Texi-cano-raised butch queen who moved to Los Angeles a year ago. An avowed heartthrob any queer femme would love to have splashed on the cover of a crotch-burning romance novel. Sebastian began to unbutton their vest and shirt. They walked shirtless to the small pyramid pile of soil that sat north of the gallery and took a bit of the earthen dust, rubbing it on their hands. Holier than water. Sebastian fell to their knees and crawled slowly around the space, their torso elongated with each stretch, each movement accentuating muscle and rib cage. Sebastian then stopped and sat down, not quite cross-legged. Suddenly, a knife appeared in my sight line and Sebastian pulled their right foot toward their body and proceeded to use the blade on another object of Tejano authenticity—the black leather cowboy boots. Sebastian relentlessly worked the knife back and forth across the heel. The sound of leather tearing rung out. It felt endless. This was a durational performance art event with a predominantly hetero-Tejano audience that glowered at Sebastian. They finally made progress with the gutting of the boot, splitting it open like a lizard's belly, exposing their black-socked foot. Nothing casts the demons of rejection out like a flagrant dismantling of cocksure masculinity.

San Cha had flown in a few days earlier and was absolutely glorious in a floor-length, Frida blue dress with hummingbird appliqués and winged epaulets, her hair slicked back in a femme ducktail. It was going to be a solo serenata performance, with San Cha strumming her acoustic guitar, a modest sized bottle of Corralejo Reposado at her feet.

I was filled with the ecstatic possibility that the traditional San Antonio crowd was not ready for San Cha's Califas-chaos-imbued cumbias and torch song ranchera numbers. Originally from San Jose, California, home of Los Tigres Del Norte, San Cha (real name Lizette Anabelle Gutierrez) and I both lived in San Francisco from around 2013 to 2015. We never connected there yet her hustle was familiar to me. It was hard being an artist in San Francisco, and for that I will never forgive the city. She left her multiple part-time gigs and insufficient wage jobs for better pastures down south—first at her family's ranch in a small Jalisco hamlet and then in Los Angeles, where she continues to be the jewel of its queer underground, playing to crowds who can't get enough of her devastating cumbia originals and punk rock interpretations of modern Spanish-language classics. My first proper witnessing of San Cha's beguiling performance had taken place a few years earlier at the First Street Pool and Billiard Parlor in Boyle Heights. San Cha played rhythm guitar on an old Fender Stratocaster and, backed by Oscar Santos and the queerest band of noisemakers this side of the Los Angeles River, played joint after hot joint for a cross-section of East Los aging punks, millennial deejays, and Gen Z club kids. The place was divey and timeless in that trapped amber kind of way where you knew the place would cease to exist, just as recreational sites were always the first to lose in the battle over a barrio's soul. It was a perfect debut in the new city she would call home.

San Cha's rendition of "Los Laureles" summoned the spirit of Lola Beltran. She electrified the room with a voice as indelible as Beltran's and stunned the audience into delayed waves of applause. I felt a pride swell up in me and maybe some Southern Californian snobbishness. Our artists were going to demonstrate to this San Antonio audience how precisely it is us who can scare them into feeling something. It is our talent that inoculates dignity into the pain of being cast out from the warm tendrils of family and cultural recognition.

San Cha had warmed up the crowd and now it felt like the party had finally climaxed. I was able to get my energy charge by way of hugs, kisses, and tequila shots with San Cha, rafa, and Sebastian. We were four brown queers from Los Angeles in San Antonio, spirited away, back up to rafa's upstairs loft apartment for a quick huddle about what we were collectively witnessing downstairs.

Is it me or would people have lost their shit over you guys if we were in L.A.?

This place was only a hundred miles from Crystal City, Texas, the real birthplace of the Chicano movement. I always felt sheepish when I remember those of us from East Los who claimed the walkouts as if they didn't occur in Texas first. This is the reckoning of a bad education. The Chicano pursuit of civil rights was a history worth hijacking to craft an identity, an aesthetic provision for a covetous representation. An identity based on a radical politic, and now we're including queerness and rejection of the heteropatriarchy. We just want to be seen so we're bearing it all.

There's always going to be a push and pull between us—Californios and Tejanos. And our aesthetics. It's a familiar violence that manifests in the strange policing that emerges when two sides of a coin join in temporary gathering. We make fun of each other's foodways and the styles with which we code ourselves. Is that what families do? But it's the unspoken critique of the other and the culture of whiteness we latch onto that registers when we step foot into each other's habitus. The twang of *y'all* and the laidback *órale*—the ways in which we ignore the stoner cadence of too many Cheech and Chong references and the Caló we have dismissed in our pursuit of more suitable and less masculinist aesthetics.

The four of us were a fair sample of those who grew up either in SoCal or as the children of Mexican immigrants during the gubernatorial era of Pete Wilson and his toxic worship of the Reaganism free market death cult; we were the lot last night who grew up on dispatches from Insurgente Marcos and Comandante Ramona in the Lacandon jungle of Chiapas following the Zapatista uprising in 1994. We got tear-gassed while headbanging to Rage Against the Machine's performance at the 2000 Democratic National Convention in the parking lot of the Staples Center. We did Arena, Circus, Tempo, Chico, and soaked up our excess at Gran Burrito on Santa Monica Boulevard at Vermont Avenue. We listened to Mark Torres's *Travel Tips to Aztlan* on KPFK Pacifica Radio. We worshipped playwright Luis Alfaro and Marisela Norte, the unofficial poet laureate of East Los Angeles. And we witnessed the son jarocho purity wars of the mid 2010s between Quetzal and Las Cafeteras. We danced all night and we fucked our friends and we went to breakfast as our serotonin levels dropped to the floor and back again.

The four of us were brought up in the immigrant friendly-enough cradle of blue state California, taking a queer night in and out of red Texas. Over a few shots of San Cha's half empty bottle of tequila, rafa, Sebastian, San Cha, and I chattered about our experiences as children of Mexican immigrants being encouraged, sometimes celebrated, and never encroached upon in our late twentieth century upbringings. Sebastian's parents were danzantes, teaching Sebastian and their siblings to honor the four directions alongside beautiful routines in Aztec-style garb and performing ceremonies from dawn to dusk for Día de Los Muertos. San Cha dove deep into the Mexican songbooks of José Alfredo Jiménez and lived in Jalisco with her grandmother as a way to escape the slow death of wage labor in the Bay Area. My own dad, who arrived in Texas, Wisconsin, and then California from Pachuca, Hidalgo, to pick potatoes, lettuce, and strawberries as a farmworker, was a businessman by the time I was born in the mid-seventies. He knew wage theft firsthand and wanted to soften the hard knocks of the young Latino and monolingual men he would contract to work for him laying brick, installing plumbing, and hanging drywall. He would offer a fair day's or week's wage, meals, beer, and references for housing. Truthfully, my father's favorite thing was to just drink and talk shit with these men.

I don't mean to build a contrarian trap here, but there is something to say about the way our encounter with the Tejano that evening is washed over by this hard-to-broach estrangement with Mexicanidad. Or rather, we are all witness to the palpable tension present when encountering the brownness in the environment born of rafa 's work, as well as the critical ethos in Sebastian's embodied performance, and San Cha's queer tequiladas reminiscent of Chavela Vargas. (San Cha's own Mexican narrative is as unsettling as Chavela Vargas's choice to disavow Costa Rica and choose Mexico, where she found her foothold as a beloved musical artist).

I also had to remember that rafa's project is not an easy one to sit beside, especially when you've lived your life striving for stability away from the violence that imbricates an existence on the stolen land of the southwest region. On the contemporary art center's walls, rafa plainly speaks of "the ways our bodies and land are targets of white supremacy and its violence."[21]

This country has excelled in creating exclusionary systems. *Maybe we're just walking into one right now. Maybe we're living in one hopped up on Adderall and Viagra.* Maybe these systems have had forty years to improve their ability to prioritize the free market and facilitate our own surveillance and call it individualism.

The last few years have been an experiment in de-Californizing myself. It fuels my desire to be in the Southwest—Arizona and Texas—and to encounter the spectrum of ways

21. From *With Land* (https://www.artpace.org/works/iair/iair_spring_2018/with-land).

that we inhabit this nebulous and suspicious category of brownness. What does brownness do to wrestle us away from national affiliations and other flattening machinations of categorization? De-Californizing myself that evening meant flirting with a Tejanx disavowal of that brownness. How might I explore the roots of that particular type of self-loathing I am familiar with, similar to aspirations toward whiteness that Texas history books teach brown kids. Am I seeing that energy subtly animate my encounters with Tejanos? Am I only hanging out with degreed and pedigreed aspirational brown queers? I know anecdotal evidence isn't enough. And I get the history of Mexican lynchings and the violence of the Texas Rangers on the Mexican psyche and how, over time, that will make one reach for the basket of white bread on a dinner table over tortillas. Or remember the scoldings in front of your classmates for speaking Spanish. These violences are cyclical. Finding your history and culture and literature on a banned books list will do it, too. It may emerge in increments and in different parts of our depressive impulses, but we are all great at castigating and policing ourselves. I didn't speak Spanish to my parents all throughout high school. I didn't want to until I went to my first Los Crudos show and heard the music in Martín Sorrondeguy's Spanish-language narration of the Latin American freedom movements that served as inspirations for each song.

Don't let your takeaway be that only Tejanos excel at self-loathing—these are the modes of denial that traverse our politically constructed state lines. White supremacy is the norm, and the best white supremacists are often the ones with Spanish surnames.

It was the end of the opening and we left ArtPace for the guest house where I would be staying. I dropped off my suitcase and settled into my room before heading to where Risa, the curator and homegrown San Antonian, was staying. We were in the popular King William District, the arts center adjacent to downtown. It's a familiar scene—coffee shops, breweries, gastropubs with their exposed brick and wooden beams, another upcycled neighborhood that has pushed through its own skin. Risa brought us to a house I had been to before, many years ago, through another friend, the arts educator Annele Spector, who brought me for a party with locals. That party was crowded with aging cowpunks, armchair anarchists, street artist types and ne'er-do-wells that I had much simpatico with, myself an ever-aspirational dirtbag who could find intimacies with the strangest of strangers. I remembered a missing plank in the kitchen floor on the way to the bathroom and an abundance of futons, indoors and out. And falling in love with Lone Star beer.

Tonight's party was different—populated by the college-educated, the autodidacts, the patrons, the benefactors, the art-schooled. And the middle-aged dilettantes and recovered punks finding new ways of self-employment—the house flipper, the nascent tech bro, the trust funded, the food justice activist, and several performance artists. The rosé was flowing.

The cryptomnesia of that dwelling nagged at me, making me too aware of the palimpsestic crux of a place's convivial history and potentiality. Its future was mapped out in familiar ways. It was another reminder of the ways I have consumed my identity over the course of my adulthood. The constrictions of debt made it impossible to strive for collective action to dismantle the capitalist systems that didn't simply oppress me—they bored me. Nonstop accumulation of wealth meant no time for pursuing various vagaries for connection. My misery lived for company. Anything to delay my spirit entering a living vegetative state. And the site of that night's party was where flights of fancy had come to die and be reborn into commodities.

The five of us had rolled up to this house and immediately split up to find our respective vices. I circulated through the backyard, which was lit up beautifully with string lights and neon lights on the shed. The backyard was immense and seemed to be shared between four houses on a lot. It had no fencing, which felt like a hopeful signal that those who lived here might value something other than private property. I caught a young woman holding up her iPhone to snap a shot of the neon sign on the shed. And the rosé had done its job when I called her attention and asked if it was hard to photograph the neon at night. I had taken plenty of smartphone photographs of neon over the last few years and knew the ghostly streaks caused by moving your phone suddenly, or losing the legibility of the text without enough light. I had caught her off guard, self-conscious of the Instagram post interruptus.

I'm sorry, I didn't mean to interrupt your social media post. But also, your dress is amazing. I was teasing and I was serious—her dress was a colorful, eighties-era Meso-American-patterned multiverse in maximalism. And this woman's eyes flashed in that way that signaled she was down to play.

What are you? She didn't mean my ethnic background. We did the astrological info swap and proceeded to guess each other's ages terribly. I guessed thirty and she guessed fifty and we both laughed *ouch!* S was San Antonio-born and Stanford-bred—I never understood why high achievers were drawn to me, moth to flame. Our back-and-forth flirtation was going off like a firing squad when her tall and lanky boyfriend rolled in to fetch her. We did not say good-bye in that way that illuminates millennial social norms. We retracted quietly to our respective corners.

San Antonio didn't feel like a queer city but a gay and lesbian one where people have eschewed promiscuity for marriage. Gay marriage was legalized in Texas in June 2015 and three years later the honeymoon in Texas was still going strong. This is what makes me unlikably Californian—to have had this thing since 2011 and have automatically rejected it, not wanting to partake in an institution built on the stability of shared property accumulation. It's beyond taking the opportunity for granted.

I spotted Sebastian, eyes flashing over the cloud on their face. We were both teetering on a glamorous rage, smiling through gritted teeth. Back in boy drag and swishing their agave spirit in their plastic cup as they politely kept attention on the local gay performance artist who also had a piece in the exhibition. This was my first trip in half a decade and the first time I was introduced to peoples' wives and husbands. *Don't people just fuck anymore?* I whispered to Sebastian. We were both between and over the idea of commitment, so naturally we linked arms and walked over to the center of the yard where several picnic tables stood, our kin sitting and gathering around San Cha, who had been strumming her guitar—a different, smaller instrument than the one she had played in the gallery. She smiled impishly and batted her eyelashes as she regaled us with song. I was losing my shit. The intimacy of this queer serenata, an homage to where the many hearts of the Tejano music world converge. San Cha started playing the familiar chords of Selena's "Si Una Vez," but in a quicker tempo which was, of course, pretty punk. We sang along, our voices rising in harmony. San Cha played an extended version. Then we were shushed by an older white man in a seersucker suit that signaled to me that he was possibly one of the owners of the several homes surrounding the green space. One of us croaked, *oops,* and the white man nodded his head and smiled sheepishly, perhaps trusting that we might adhere to his caution. Before the man could walk away out of earshot San Cha started strumming faster and scream-singing as the rest of us broke into hysterical laughter. *Pinche viejo.*

Baby Themme Anthems:
The Werq of Sebastian Hernández

2019 | "Everytime" by Britney Spears has haunted me since my friend Sebastian chose it as the opening number for their workshop presentation of *Hypanthium,* an ensemble multimedia performance that is, at its heart, a portrait of an artist as a young themme.[22] In late January I was preparing to attend the work's full-length debut, curious to see how the *Hypanthium* had evolved since its workshop presentation last summer. Britney's baby piano and little girl howl opens a short three-minute film shot by rafa (one of Sebastian's longtime collaborators) portraying Sebastian, scantily clad, running in a disoriented manner up and down the 4th Street bridge where Boyle Heights leads into downtown. The song is mashed up against a bit of spoken word from a pair of distinct sources—a poem colliding aurally with a broadcast news headline about Trump. It's a cacophony signaling a meditation on queer, brown precarity—or what it means for femme-identified Sebastian to live in a time of complete uncertainty. The film offers Sebastian

---

22. A themme is a resilient creature or a nonbinary femme, sometimes both and seldom mutually exclusive.

wrapped in pink cellophane ribbons, careening against the early evening canvas in high, hot-pink heels, with leather straps winding around their muscular calves like a fashionable gladiator when the song opens.

The camera pans eastward and westward toward a setting sun over a downtown skyline. Sebastian balances on the edge of the 4th Street bridge overlooking the Los Angeles river, averting the specter of societal disaster on the streets of downtown, forecasting a new Los Angeles we struggle to recognize, both they and the city awash in the magical hour's heavenly light.

The song and the brown subjectivity under duress that it animates feel like a message from the queer future that, in these dangerous conditions, feels further and further away.

Prepping a trip to Los Angeles from Tucson has conjured the piano pop ballad back to me as I've been thinking about Sebastian's oeuvre. I'm obsessing—why this song?

Sebastian's from my hometown of Huntington Park, a municipality seven miles south of downtown Los Angeles, a place that invites its inhabitants to lose their softness in exchange for survival. Sebastian is tough—that queen who can do everything you can do but backward, wearing patent leather high heel boots and Dickies. Their candy-colored ribbons, intimidatingly thorny long-stemmed roses, and Made-in-China, disposable, brightly hued plastics have helped shape their court in the various performance works I've caught them doing in venues such as the Human Resources Gallery in Los Angeles's Chinatown. Seeing Sebastian perform their first top billed performance at one of the most respected venues in town made my heart swell with pride. But tethering Sebastian's brand of femme furious performance art to the deceptively cloying vulnerability of Britney's ballad gave me pause until I listened again. And again. And I am flooded with the memory of the theater darkening and the familiar sight of a Los Angeles cityscape and Sebastian's blurry figure brought to life by the Britney selection, and seeing them again. And again. I feel invited into a dream realm permeated with a femme vulnerability, pulsating inside the creative walls—an artistic hypanthium, if you will—that hold Sebastian's own performative nectaries.

I suddenly feel the optics adjust in myself when I see them back up again on the theater's screen.

In 2004, when the song was released, I still hadn't figured out how queer artists of color could take back what was stolen by Britney's predecessors. I loved Madonna even as she snatched my soul. But gleaning the cultural nuances of gendered performativity thanks to a degreed dalliance with performance studies means I'm listening now with new ears. Maybe it's queer aging or having assimilated those queer brown butch life lessons that has given me the gift of middle-aged lesbian longevity. It's why I am now able to heed the song's unabashed call for softness and forgiveness, delivered through Spears's seductive yet exhausted girl-on-the-verge whisper. While it may have been Britney's rebuttal to her ex Justin Timberlake's indicting "Cry Me a River," for me it's a baby themme anthem for a mean ol' butch daddy queering the lyrics to Joni Mitchell's "Carey." A mean ol' daddy who's losing interest in being mean these days, opting for moving and grooving to club queens, crooning over four-four house beats, and slowing down enough to let the ballad set the pace.

Whether it's the dance floor at Chico's in Montebello or Mustache Mondays in downtown, I've shared many a dance or a knowing glance with Sebastian, who's twirled me elegantly into the twilight of our respective nightlives. I've learned how to move better—how to glide, wring, and dab my body to the music, take up space elegantly for once. How to float accordingly, to surrender my toxic masculinities as the anchors that hinders my growth, my curiosity of self. I have forgone the trappings of the binary—the dreariness of plaid, the explanatory impulses of patriarchal masculinity, a reluctance toward intimacy. Instead, I have rediscovered reinvention and have made it a new rite of passage back into my softer parts. Sebastian models those passages with aplomb and without apology. I have received those blessings from Sebastian. What I have given them in return—well, that verdict is still out. All I know is that I have been making space in my wings for them, a young, queer, femme-identified gender renegade who models the finer points of extending ourselves out to one another, may softness be our code.

I don't bother to mention any of this over an extended Thanksgiving break in Los Angeles when I catch up with Sebastian, who has just started rehearsals for the January show. I reckon Sebastian has better things to obsess over as I pick them up at their family's house, situated on one of the few one-way streets in Huntington Park, a police car parked across the street a few houses away, lights on but no one in sight. The one-ways have long been the inconvenience meant to disrupt the underground economies that are the block-by-block gang rivalries. They dot the peripheries around Pacific Boulevard, the main drag in Huntington Park affectionately named "Little Tijuana" (or Little TJ). Pacific Boulevard always hits the news when Mexico wins a match in the World Cup or when the Lakers take home the championship. Little do people know it's the premier, one-stop shop for quinceañeras and brides-to-be on a budget, as well as trans femmes and club kids. Los callejones, but make it fashion.[23]

Sebastian quickly opens the passenger side of my old 4Runner and slides into the seat, giving me a quick peck on the cheek. They're wearing a dark oversized denim jacket, black jeans, and work boots—a Southeast L.A. camouflage. We are essentially twinning, except Sebastian has glass-cutting cheekbones and a tightly coiffed mustache sitting pretty on their full lips. Our body types give away clearly that they're the dancer and I'm the writer. Yet we are two brown queers performing two very distinct types of fragile masculinity, easily broken should either one of us decide to resist its various commodifications, or just turn down the wrong corner.

They lead me through a Huntington Park that is as much theirs as it is mine, as they still live there and I lived there as a toddler and sporadically for the last fourteen years, having moved away finally in 2016 for Tucson. Sebastian doesn't drive and urges me to go against my cocksure shortcuts through Huntington Park's warehouse corridor. *What's the tea?* I deadpan as I take all of Vernon Avenue to Central, shaving ten minutes off our commute to downtown. Sebastian narrates their new romantic entanglement for me, but this time the crush has a career implication. That's how I confirm Sebastian's on the verge of blowing up. These are great problems that test discipline against desire, I tell them. They roll their eyes. We find Kojak parking for a semi-quick bowl of pho before a reading I'm participating in to celebrate our friend Nikki's new novel. I spill my tea to Sebastian—my ex and I have been mutually creeping on one another via the social media platform du jour.

---

23. "The allies," in reference to Santee Alley in Downtown Los Angeles, where bargain shopping for brand-name knockoffs is popular with Latinxs.

This would be normalized, except Sebastian reminds me I'm over forty and thus what the fuck am I doing? I tell them my ex just left her rebound relationship and moved back to Tucson. Sebastian puts the hurt on me. *This career queer is not going to come back for your ass.* Ouch.

You and my mom are the meanest Sagittarians I know, I say as I slurp my beef pho, a wounded silence setting in, and I remember how hard it sometimes is to be with family.

———

Born in Los Angeles to immigrants from the state of Mexico, Sebastian came into movement as a family affair—their parents and siblings all danced traditional Aztec folklórico, a dance project often realized on Catholic and national holidays, an Indigenous response for a people still reeling from colonization's persistent toll, a dance to remind us that indigeneity often reveals itself through joyful movement, through community performances. Sunrise ceremonies take place every Thanksgiving, for example, when Aztec danzantes greet the darkened sky with an offering of mourning, a set of choreographed dances timed with the rise of the morning sun.

As part of their performance art, Sebastian's danzante work has shaped collaborative performances they have done with rafa. In 2014, the two performed *no water under the bridge* under the 4th Street Viaduct in East Los Angeles. Sebastian donned their danzante garb, with feathers and glittered vestments made to look like animal pelts, and took their seemingly inexhaustible turn with durational performance while rafa initiated a series of movements in response to Sebastian's choreography. The work is a blood ritual for young brown men lost to urban violence. The two artists describe the iconic viaduct on 4th Street and Lorena in Boyle Heights as a site in which "popular films, such as *Mi Familia, Blood in Blood Out,* and *Colors,* have explored the intersection of history, violence, gang culture, the industrial prison complex, and Chicanidad. These films have helped construct internationally recognized identities/stereotypes of Latinos/as living in Los Angeles." Both rafa and Sebastian have long reckoned with these stereotypes, grinding them into a wearable material that conjures the burden of a Chicano identity, a Chicano gender, slipping from its post in the East Los Angeles context that grounded them, where they have imagined the "space between their self-identifications and projected identities from an unknown public gaze." The performance lasted more than two hours.

Durational performance as a practice has instilled in Sebastian a palpable discipline that resonates with audiences that grow larger with each new presentation of their work, especially since 2018, when they performed their own solo

compositions in both Los Angeles and San Antonio. But durational performance as a device also warrants attention for the
performance of masculinity that has exhausted Sebastian into
new realizations about how their gender complicates both inte-
rior and material realities as an artist living and making work
for a gender-conscious and laudatory Los Angeles while living
in gender-prohibitive Huntington Park. A Huntington Park
that demands its denizens to ride its buses to work each day, to
amble down its crosswalks toward and away from one another
in gender costumes that adhere to the sex one is assigned at
birth—whether that birth was in California or Mexico or
Guatemala. Sebastian is, in many ways, asking us what we are
enduring when we put on a gender that makes each one of us
both legible and invisible to each other.

———

Artists like Marina Abramović and Tehching Hsieh are the
avatars of performance art for our contemporary moment.
So present is performance art in the cultural imaginary that
I can see *The Simpsons* dragging into the town of Springfield
Abramović's notorious performative, eye-gazy, soul-charging
persona from *The Artist Is Present*. And why not? The animated
series recently featured America's favorite dysfunctional family
driving through another art center, Marfa, Texas. But what is
performance art exactly? I have never been able to define it
with any single, precise description. Many performance
artists define their genre through action and a sense of the
temporal and temporary, rather than through a permanent
artistic gesture that starts and then finishes. But there is more
to that. For Abramović, performance "is the moment when
the performer with his own idea steps into his own mental,

physical construction [of that idea] in front of the audience." For Abramović the blood and knife are real, whereas in theater they are not. For fans and scholars of performance art, we hope that there can be documentation of the performance—from photos and objets d'art to full video documentation that provide access to the history of performance art, but the performance itself resides in the space of ephemerality and is reanimated through engagements with the archive. But sometimes we are actually there, in the audience, getting our minds blown by witnessing the utmost distillation of liveness. Being there to see it as it was meant to be seen is key. And as someone who has seen her fair share of performance art, and has spent time poring over texts and theories about the range of expressions present in the form, I hover over the space of the durational. The durational as it lives and exists in the repetition of movements, Sebastian's movements, is speaking to me about what it means to wear our bodies in the street, on the stage, in our bedrooms. It is the durational embedded in performance art that allows for a porous exhibition and examination of endurance, the body utilizing all it has to make visible an attempt toward a psychological mastery over pain, solitude, exhaustion, and fear. It is in the durational that the artist gives us—their witnesses—an embodied representation of the ways we all endure the spectrum of difficult feelings customized to and for our material realities.

In some ways this is how I would define trauma. The obsessive rehearsal of the initial wound and refusal to release the concomitant humiliations that endure hauntologically. We need this pain to live. It becomes the story that holds attention. I have often sought a replication of such punishments. It keeps others attached to me. I wouldn't recognize myself outside of such imbrication. These are the familiar contours that comfort me. And rehearsing these scripts make them just legible enough for those who want to protect me, bear witness, or offer presence.

Abramović and Hsieh both have centered their own bodies in work that demanded a range of punishing acts spanning hours, days, weeks, and years. *Art must be Beautiful, Artist must be Beautiful* is one of Abramović's typical early performances, in which the artist takes a brush and violently runs it through her long hair while reciting that "art must be beautiful" for almost an hour on video. Hsieh has performed each of his works for one year at a time. His best known, *One Year Performance 1978–1979 (Cage Piece)*, featured him living inside a wooden cage for a year before moving to different yearlong endeavors that cemented his place as a master of durational art. Another of these yearlong performances, *Time Clock Piece (One Year Performance 1980–1981)*, featured Hsieh punching a time clock every hour for a year.[24] The durational elements of their respective bodies of work have defined an important form of performance art for Los Angeles artists in recent years.

Since 2001, Los Angeles with its cheaper-than-New-York rents, has become an underground center of durational art, with artists arriving from the East Coast, mingling with the locally born and bred, and together raising sufficiently passable resources to make new work on their own terms and in their own artist-run venues. These collaborations lead to artists connecting with curators who present their work in such venues as Los Angeles Contemporary Exhibitions in Hollywood, which often serves as the stepping-stone to larger museum venues, such as the Hammer Museum in Westwood. Artists

---

24. Tehching Hsieh, *One Year Performance: 1980–1981,* https://www.tate.org .uk/art/artworks/hsieh-one-year-performance1980-1981-t13875.

like rafa have animated endurance work with new contextual framing around race, immigration status, violence, and homophobia—issues that have brought about a cross-sector (and cross-pollination) of audiences that go beyond Los Angeles counties. Rafa and collaborators like Sebastian, San Cha, and Gabriela Ruiz have made names for themselves while enabling the city itself to hold a new place in the annals (as well as the imaginary) of contemporary art.

————

I finally got the chance to work with Sebastian a couple of years ago on an exhibition I co-curated for a small community gallery in San Pedro, California, on the Los Angeles harbor. The exhibition was called *Coastal/Border*. According to my catalog essay (that no one read) *Coastal/Border* was:

> *an experiment grounded in a critical recovery of minoritarian narratives reperformed by the six artists invited to create, through a range of decolonializing impulses that look at the histories that contribute to the contemporary issues that we can read into the landscape as it is taken apart. To say the minimal, these performances will expose how transnational material realities have impacted communities of color situated in close and conceptual proximities to the Port of Los Angeles. To say it at maximal level, however, is why we arrive to the Coastal/Border. It is here where we gather around the state-making tensions that undergird this exhibition of performance. In various forms and configurations, we have spent the last two years calling into question the tendencies to call on the colonial mythologies unique to Coastal California*

as both historical shorthanded and shortchanged amnesia evidenced in the spatial politics of Fort MacArthur and Cabrillo Beach in San Pedro, the harbor city of Los Angeles County.

I was proud of the exhibition but, most of all, grateful that it gave me a chance to finally get to know Sebastian. I've found in my life—coming in and out of the various doors and rooms that art has housed me in—that it's always these collaborative opportunities that allow me to really know a person. With Sebastian, I got a sense of their desire to bridge the myriad endurances of everyday life. As two brown queers—adult children of mainly monolingual immigrants—we mirror each other's psychological portraits to some degree. We see each other's psychic excess which, to put it plainly, is just us being ourselves. No code-switching to appease the spatial contexts that hold us. We are in mutual appreciation of each other's trauma and our demystification of that trauma. We are father and daughter, mother and son. We are rough and elegant at the same time. We harness our psychological leaks in order to spill them over the borders that attempt to hold those excesses—inside our bodies, sometimes our barrios, sometimes both in strangely interchangeable ways.

For *Coastal/Border,* Sebastian proposed *FTZ (Free/Foreign Trade Zone),* a performance happening, text, and installation work concerned with contamination. Sebastian and I would get together at the Mexi-hipster café spot on Pacific Boulevard and talk through concepts of contamination as we combed through many of Leonard Nadel's photographs of Mexican migrants coming to work in the u.s. through the Bracero Program. In the fifties, Nadel documented the Bracero Program for the Ford Foundation's Fund for the Republic, producing searing images of the Mexican Guest Worker program that endured from 1942 to 1964. These photographs were taken in connection with a survey of braceros done by Ernesto Galarza, a man of letters who emigrated to California from Nayarit, Mexico, to work in the fields as a child. He became both a labor organizer and activist, returning to Central California after completing his doctorate from Columbia University in 1944. Nadel's photographs illustrate the issues Galarza wrote about in his publication, *Strangers in Our Fields.* During World War II, the u.s. and Mexico entered a farm labor agreement to offset the u.s. wartime labor shortage by importing braceros (from the term *brazo,* meaning "arm," or those who work with their arms). The war ended but the bracero program continued through the early sixties, and by the time of Nadel's photographs almost 500,000 Mexican contract workers were legally allowed to work on u.s. agricultural farms, mostly on short-term labor contracts that paid workers thirty cents an hour, considered a fair wage at the time. The workers were known as "dry-backs," a take on the derogatory term "wetback," suggesting that these Mexicans didn't have to swim across the Rio Grande to get to u.s. soil. Being called "dry-backs," however, is just one of the

many indignities these Mexicanos endured as temporary workers upon arriving in the United States. As many of Nadel's
photographs show, the most disturbing indignities involved
group bodily inspections and fumigation with toxic chemicals
before entering the U.S.

While these images unabashedly document the undeni-
ably exploitative conditions these men endured in pursuit of
higher U.S. wages, for Sebastian, they also offered an opportunity to create an embodied choreographic dialogue with
the ways in which brown masculine sexuality is displayed.
Nadel composed many of his photographs chronicling this
important period of mid-twentieth-century U.S. labor history
with the Mexican masculine body, often nude, in groups of
other nude Mexican torsos and bodies, being searched and
scrutinized in such a way that imputes a sinister eros onto
the images. Or at least that's what happens with our queer
brown gaze. That queerness can exist in the more degrading
corners of American history is a concern Sebastian takes up
in their work. Sebastian mentioned to me over our cloyingly
sweet horchata lattes just how Nadel's images paralleled their
own experience with being subjected to forms of contamination control. Sebastian has felt the intersection of gay cis
male cultural expectations and market imperative in the pressure to go on PrEP because they are perceived as someone
at very high risk for contracting HIV—a brown femme body
from a working-class, immigrant-dominant barrio called
Huntington Park. A barrio peopled by those with minimal to
no access to healthcare. The Centers for Disease Control has
said that a pre-exposure prophylaxis (or PrEP) when taken
daily lowers the chances of getting infected.

As a genderqueer, fluid femme interventionist who makes
visible the fraught relationship with a body assigned otherwise

at birth, Sebastian wants to fuck shit up. They situate their embodied subjectivity as a counterpoint to the kind of low-grade surveillance carried out by the pharmaceutical industry—no one wants to be cruised at the club and asked their PrEP status right out of the gate. *Like, I get it, but don't lead with it if you're trying to step to me,* they snap.

———

The most visibly captivating of objects driving Sebastian's *FTZ* is the cactus plant. The cactus is one of the most identifiable succulent plant species, taking various forms along the political borders between the United States and Mexico, most notably in the deserts of the Southwest. It is indefatigable, able to weather sweltering heat and recognized by border dwellers and crossers as a natural physical marker indicating that the demarcation of north and south is close. It is an object that brings awareness to the stark materiality of a bordered landscape that the Indigenous, Mexican, and Latinx migrants know or are at least familiar with in varied and intimate ways. Their histories, ancient and recent, are witnessed by the saguaros and opuntias that live side by side, a demarcation that separates people from those histories. By installing a nopal plant in the gallery, Sebastian gestures to a need for a phenomenologic of care, an anticipated instruction for nurturance, for softness toward the nopal's requisite self-protection. This simple act, however, also offers the nopal—the cactus plant—as a symbol that calls our attention to the complicated relationship to brownness and the identity markings connected to Latinidad, Indigeneity, and the ways those markings of belonging are inscribed on the artist's brown body. Sebastian's cactus conceptual orchestration is forcing constructions of Latinidad and Indigeneity to reckon with each other. This reckoning, a prickly encounter where an elision of identity categories has no space to speak, brings to mind the folk metaphor "con el nopal en la frente," lodged as a critical adage specifically at individuals of Mexican descent living in the U.S. who have assimilated readily, which requires a casting off of anything remotely "Mexican." Awkwardly translated to "with the cactus on his forehead," the nopal in this vernacular register is used to punish the darker-skinned Mexican with Indigenous physical traits who claim not to know Spanish or the customs belonging to Mexican culture. This betrayal is read as the absolute affront to cultural nationalists, especially those lighter-skinned Mexicanos who aren't just passing for white.

And I'm tripping because I'm a lighter shade of brown, a legible Latinx with more pronounced Spanish features (have you seen my hairy arms?), feeling the rush of blood flush my cheeks, feeling the indictment and invitation to question my own anti-Indigenous rhetorics with which I've been raised. For Sebastian, though, the nopal as incendiary castigating object is brought into the gallery space to invert the pejorative charge by offering it as a petition for an ethics of care for the brown femme body, one that animates another of Sebastian's concurrent projects that they manage via their browncommonz Instagram account. The title is an homage to the work of the late José Muñoz, whose electrifying essay "The Brown Commons: The Sense of Wildness" is one of the multiple essays in a posthumous collection of Muñoz's work on affect theories of brown ontology titled *The Sense of Brown*. Muñoz begins his essay (read in front of an academic audience at Eastern Michigan University in the spring of 2013) by describing a commons of "brown people, places, feelings, sounds, animals, minerals, and other objects . . . how these things are brown or what makes them brown is partially in the way they suffer and stride together but also the commonality in their ability to flourish under duress and pressure ... in part because they have been devalued by a world outside of their commons."[25]

Sebastian raises the stakes of Muñoz's evocative call with their work by documenting the Los Angeles–specificity of a brown commons, which is important to their quotidian thinking and process as ways to forge an artistic practice contingent on demonstrating the simultaneity of flourishing and duress, beauty in the face of devaluement. These flourishings and devaluement can exist in parallel contexts—queer and hegemonic demonstrations of brown masculinity can coexist in and beyond the labor structures that call those masculinities into place as sources of labor, especially within the sociopolitical space of Southeast Los Angeles. However, in their almost contraband act of documenting a community (whether it's Pacific Boulevard in Southeast Los Angeles's Huntington Park or the commuter buses that crisscross downtown Los Angeles traffic) they bring into our purview the high risk Sebastian places themselves in as a chronicler whose gender and embodiment may potentially be read and responded to violently. Sebastian, in their contribution to *Coastal/Border,* presents this quandary by utilizing nopals as material for both installation and the object for a performance mask (a "cara de nopal"). A way to both hide from and mess with a machismo that hinders their own sense of belonging to a brown commons they are actively seeking out on social media. The kind of machismo that puts Sebastian in real, physical danger. Which might be the same

25. "JNT Dialogue 2013: José Muñoz and Samuel Delany (Part 1/4)." April 1, 2013, www.youtube.com/watch?v=F-YInUlXgO4.

kind of machismo that turns them on. Putting on a cactus mask lets Sebastian play with machismo's meaning safely, but the cactus still pricks.

————————

I left Tucson early on the second Friday of December to see Sebastian's performance component for *FTZ*. It was scheduled to be the closing event for *Coastal/Border*. It took all day to get to Los Angeles, whereas past excursions between my two homes clocked in at under eight hours on the road, stops for gas included. Today, of all days, my car decided to break down, the engine wheezing its last breath fewer than twenty miles from the nearest gas station. My worst nightmare as a desert denizen is to break down on the highways in the middle of the desert, miles away from the nearest sign of help, stuck in the signal-less ethers rendering my phone a useless technology—my gender, my sex, and my ethnicity putting me at risk in the pastoral hinterlands of my adopted town. As I'm waiting for the tow truck to come and find me, I think about the Carlos Almaraz car crash paintings I had seen over Thanksgiving break at LACMA. The explosions of automobiles in a meeting between Van Gogh's violent strokes and Repo Man's velocity, the Los Angeles of my youth in the background, concrete and palm trees, traffic and smoggy sunsets. I'm remembering the lore behind these paintings—the artist's premonitions of a premature death through these visions, shared with his psychoanalyst who gently suggested he merely paint them. Maybe that would somehow diminish Almaraz's propensity toward a legible self-annihilation at the hands of a killer no one would have thought twice about, since everyone in Los Angeles traverses as part of a death drive that goes with the flow of traffic.

In this IRL version of the nightmare, though, it's only fifty degrees, not in the middle of some scorch-storm of summer, and my phone works fine. And I reach a towing service willing to spirit me away to safety for two hundred dollars. My car of fourteen years though, trusty steed and witness to my elusive adulthood, is knocking on death's door, and I am thankful that my tow truck driver is nice enough—a gruff-voiced Santa Claus type with an American flag air freshener dangling from the rearview. We talk cars and bond over a mutual love for late sixties model Ford Rancheros, an early prototype for the El Camino. I thank my San Francisco femme friends' vehicular enthusiasm in my mind and take it all as a good sign that cacti whir alongside the truck and that my nervous system feels calm, intact. Once I leave the car with a mechanic in Glendale, Arizona, where it will stay forever, I decide to get a rental car and continue onward to Los Angeles.

———

The next day I wake up in the guest bedroom at my parents' new house in Downey, California, where they are busy getting ready for Christmas. They are both in their mid-seventies and exuding a radiance I hadn't ever known before. Or not when they lived in Huntington Park. My mom and dad were happier? Happier to be in the town they always saw as several steps up from Huntington Park, where they felt vulnerable as they settled into the twilight of their lives. They used to live next-door to a family affiliated with the 18th Street gang—evident when the garage door was tagged with large, black, spray-painted Roman numerals after they were evicted by their landlord.

I swallow some coffee and a pastry, yell good-bye to my mom as I head out the door, and hit the road again, this time to

San Pedro. The performance is scheduled for two in the afternoon, but I arrive at eleven to make sure Sebastian has someone from the exhibition management team present to receive them and their team. I don't work for the nonprofit gallery, but for a fifteen-hundred-dollar stipend and eighteen months of engagement, collaboration, and production as a contracted curator, I'm called upon to be there. I want to be there for Sebastian but I'm also trying to melt the butter of resentment I feel toward the organization for paying me so little for the amount of time I have given them (the space). But that's often what it takes to get artists like Sebastian their due resources to make new work, to experiment. In a Malcolm Gladwell world, I'm a connector archetype, so organizations often hire me to get them to the queer, young, brown talent while they're cheap. It has been maddening working like this, coming out of community art settings and not profiting from nonprofits. I have always tried to shield artists from the weeds of this humiliation, the sense-dulling bureaucratic violence. I take a deep breath and recalibrate for the occasion, remembering that at least the location is stunning. The gallery is located on top of a bluff overlooking the Pacific and today the sun is peeking out behind billowy white clouds, a sky so cerulean it hurts me into poetry. The performance space is an old military barrack converted to a dance studio, with long vertical windows drawing in both light and ocean air to create the most optimal space for a queer and brown artistic intervention. Our barrack sits among other converted barracks that house painting studios and other gallery spaces.

Such a perfect day, I sing quietly to myself as I set up a little green room space with water, beer, tequila, and salty liquor store snacks for the talent, and some wine and water for the anticipated public. Now for Sebastian to arrive.

And they come, eyes blazing with focus. Sebastian arrives with their sister, Ashley, to set up. Ashley is soft-spoken but has the same eyes as her sibling. Intense, soft, intense, soft. They laugh audibly as they put the final touches on the tableaus, leaving objects like fruits and scissors in the corners and in the center of the space. I notice a series of plastic baggies filled with green, blue, orange, and yellow liquid. These soft sculptures are tied to each other in such a way that the only thing I can think to compare them to are rock candy swizzle sticks. They sit at the base of the columns in the large room, columns that interfere with sight lines. Sebastian has transformed the room. *Gurl, yes,* I think.

People begin to arrive. And Sebastian retreats to the back of the space. First to arrive, as always, are our friends. It's rafa, along with San Cha, and their new friend Fabian Guerrero, a tall and handsome photographer from Dallas who's making a name for himself in the tough and fickle Los Angeles art world. It's a family reunion, but for thirty minutes it's just us, which begins to unnerve me. *Where is everyone?* But I don't let anyone see me sweat. If it's a small audience, then we shall all live to tell the tale. That's what performance art is all about. Being there, regardless of the absences and because of the absences.

I'm suddenly finding myself greeting more people though—friends and acquaintances, acquaintances who shall become my friends. It's a Saturday afternoon in one of the most far-flung locales in Los Angeles County and it's being gorgeously inundated by young ones, queer ones, brown ones, femme ones, and their admirers. Sebastian's parents are here and my heart swells. Anxiety assuaged, crisis averted, we start to build critical mass. The seating is nonexistent and no one in our audience has been directed on where to sit or where to stand, but organically everyone shifts toward the periphery of the space and sits down, most of us cross-legged, along each of the walls.

And it begins.

It begins when Sebastian comes out blindfolded, a black and white paisley handkerchief folded thickly over their eyes. They wear black jeans, a black sweatshirt, and black Nike Cortez, the sneakers made popular by any kid who ever grew up in a barrio. (Ironically, the sneaker was named after the conqueror who saw to the fall of the Aztec Empire.) They look so butch, a drag so deliciously overdetermined. Sebastian glides slowly yet assuredly, arms held at forty-five-degree angles, to different parts of the space, and finally falls to their knees, where they move like a quadruped toward the objects they have left like a trail of breadcrumbs, reaching them, touching vinyl boots, moving past the bowls of fruit, and crawling from the center of the space into various spectator zones, where they clutch at ankles, calves, shins, and knees of unsuspecting but totally expectant viewers. Sebastian slowly pulls a knife, a roll of clear mailing tape, and a banana from somewhere inside their shirt and begins to wrap the banana to their arm, cutting through the tape with their teeth, then cutting through the tape with the knife, then peeling the banana, then eating the banana and offering it blindly to the person sitting closest to them. It's anxiety producing to watch because the tape pulled in one long swoop squeaks like an animal in pain, and Sebastian is jerking around with a steak knife in one hand and a mouthful of fruit, writhing around, waiting for someone to take their offering. In this instance, Sebastian doesn't know to whom they crawl, but they have a series of rituals to go through and finding a willing participant is part of the rite. Next they are on their belly, slithering diagonally across the floor, carrying an orange now taped to the inside of their wrist and crawling, sliding their body along the floor, like they were swimming and bringing that fruit to safety. Sebastian arrives at their younger sister's feet and she smiles, though obviously self-conscious; once she feels all of our eyes on her, her face flushes. But Ashley is focused on her sibling's movements, watching Sebastian jut forward their wrist, take the steak knife, and slice through the clear tape to the center of the fruit, cutting away at the rind. When Sebastian offers the wrist, not suspecting that the receiver should be their own sister, Ashley's face begins to contort and she cries, chest heaving, her mouth opens toward the orange, her hands wiping her tears from her eyes. It's incredible to watch.

FTZ continues.

And it continues.

It is a durational piece with movement. Or an hour-long solo dance performance with objects. A choreography of gender that doesn't stop, only pausing for the occasional outfit change. A choreography of genders disintegrating only to be spliced back and forth into each other, a binary deconstructed in colorful plastic gemstones, colorful high-heeled footwear, bright liquids in sandwich baggies—but it brings to mind those color-coded terrorism threat advisory scales. It brings to mind the ways federal agencies and state and local governments respond with specific actions when different levels are triggered. By color. Be they at airports or any other public facility that enables, or hinders, a queer, femme, brown body their mobility.

———

My last trip to Los Angeles to see Sebastian's full-length debut of *Hypanthium* had been easier—no breakdowns of the vehicular kind—though so much had happened. In the weeks leading up to the performance, our friend and Sebastian's mentor, Nacho Nava, had fallen ill with a strain of pneumonia that put him on life-support for three weeks.

Nacho founded, ran, and deejayed Mustache Mondays, one of the longer running nightclubs in downtown Los Angeles. Mustache was hugely popular with queer Black and brown club kids of all ages, performance artists, musicians, and anyone versed in their own experiential history of underground culture. It was a party that had outgrown various venues, finally settling in for a near decade-long Monday night residency at La Cita, a Mexican restaurant turned epicenter, as lit on the inside as it was on the outside, with five-foot neon lights shouting its name into downtown Los Angeles's visual vernacular. Anyone who took their nightlife seriously ventured out every Monday to Hill Street at the base of downtown's infamous Bunker Hill to see the likes of Robyn performing a secret midnight show, or to have their minds blown by a then-unknown rafa sculpting masks out of plaster inside a translucent cylinder just a few feet from a crowded dance floor, or to watch a young femme named Sebastian perform kinetic choreographies for femmes and the fury that binds them.

Nacho died the Friday before *Hypanthium* opened. Rafa and I had been communicating about Nacho, hoping that the San Lázaro candle would right this wrong, praying that we would never arrive at this hole-in-the-universe kind of loss. Losing the Chronos of our queer underground, the figure who swallowed his children in protective fervor—the joto maricón bear of a dad whose smile and sweaty, hairy arms held you for as long as you needed to be held, metabolizing you into the vastness of queer possibility.

Nacho.

And, oh, how this loss animates everything about Sebastian's performance. Everything, even Britney's song, takes a new shape. Everything—from the opening hard-thumping cat-walk in the club house number that felt like an eight-minute extended club mix familiar to anyone who'd ever taken a tumble trying to deathdrop at Mustache, to the last aching tableau where Sebastian and their two collaborators, Angel Acuña and Autumn Silas Randolph, become a melancholic version of the Three of Cups tarot card, arms raised in a glorious vining up the invisible tree of grief, and then back to each other, one behind another, the musical score swelling as Sebastian's mouth opens, face crumpling, to let out *un grito en luto,* a wailing so familiar to anyone who's ever let that primal scream of femininity collect its dues, taking what it is owed.

———————

Deep, deep, deep inside
Deep, deep down inside
Deep, deep, deep inside
Deep, deep down inside
Deep, deep, deep inside
Deep, deep down inside
Deep, deep, deep inside
Deep, deep down inside

It wasn't always familiar. The thumping bass, the clapping snare, the crash cymbal. The gorgeous hazing that was waiting in an ungodly queue. The glaring at the bouncer but looking like callejón couture, a working-class catwalk. The kids that lived in my old neighborhoods, who carpooled from Huntington Park and Bell, who knew the back ways to downtown through

Vernon, who looked ready to be there like it was an assignment to ace, everyone looking like they created themselves. The Hollywood Salvis who danced until their church-appropriate, long-sleeved button-ups were drenched in sweat. And then there were the thirty-somethings who had not hung up the clubbing gloves but now partied with some aesthetic theory under their belts. This was a Monday night routine. This was Mustache.

I was in that latter group. I was still a punk and dressed in secondhand J.Crew to pass as a university administrator but I deejayed for so many queer women of color events that it was impossible not to love house, disco, and techno. It's strange—I realize my generation was so haunted by genre and the self-policing energies imprinted on any of us who claimed fandom over criticism. Why else would *poseur* be so wounding?

But as a deejay and nascent music critic, I wanted to master those genres—to play the original vinyl albums and learn the production history of Sylvester's "Mighty Real," or make queer theory out of it through close listening analysis. I pulled out those records from the milk crates I took from the El Criollo, the Cuban market on Bellevue at Lafayette, in my Silver Lake apartment. I played those records for the twenty lesbians out on the second Wednesday of each month, lesbian nights I begged the old queen who managed Woody's on Hyperion Boulevard to host.

I didn't have time for that the way I did when I was a post-punk indie record vinyl junkie right out of high school, working as a turbo Coke/red-eye pre-Starbucks-era barista at Eagle's Coffee Pub and Newsstand in North Hollywood. I was spending my weekly tips at Aron's Records on Highland in Hollywood, amassing a collection of records by bands I heard on KXLU. But after graduate school almost a decade later, my musical recreational activities were compromised. I had to sell that collection to afford the move from my eight hundred-fifty-dollar, two-bedroom Silver Lake apartment to another roommate situation in Prospect Heights for twice that same amount. I returned to Los Angeles when I completed my drive-through master's degree in Performance Studies and didn't get into the program's actually funded PhD program. At the time, I could not fathom surviving the gladiator match it takes to live in New York just to stay close to the program community. José Muñoz was my advisor and urged me to apply again. But I did not have the vanity or the pedigree to strive for a creative hustle in New York City. I wasn't sure I wanted to take on the financial burden of having a glamourous, but hard, graduate student life but I couldn't admit that so I became a self-saboteur. I did not have the working-class mettle needed to succeed. State colleges and universities were referred to as "Podunk University" during a critical race theory seminar, a joke laughed at by people with whom I am still in touch. The resources I'd gained to learn performance art histories was not meager, but my podunk university undergraduate training didn't quite prepare me for post-structuralist critic school.

This advanced art degree hung low on me, like a pair of cannonballs in my sports bra. It had weakened my shot at class mobility when I returned to Los Angeles with forty thousand dollars in debt. I lost my time trying to pay off the astonishing student debt bill that came to the tune of four hundred dollars every month. And not having the time to nurture and maintain this familiar and necessary sensory pleasure to hone hard-fought critical reading is painful. As in the tech disruption of music listening apps like Spotify that make it too easy to create personalized playlists, my fealty was to the originally sequenced album. You listen to the album as the artist intended. But you needed space and money to house and support those analog technologies.

Did Steve Jobs know we would soon not have the same disposable temporality that we once did in the late twentieth century? Learning a new sensory pleasure required time I did not have. I worked now and found modes of release through curated sonic excursions through Detroit techno, Chicago house, Latin American psychedelica, and "Back That Azz Up?" I was going into personal debt alleviating the forty-hour grind by not just partying Friday through Sunday but also including Monday in that lineup.

How could any of us not be prone to trances? Have you ever heard "Lightyears" by Juan Atkins? Isn't that why we wait in the interminable line? Isn't it the repetition that keeps us there?

———

Few nightlife venues are capable of creating the conditions necessary for spiritual communing. But this was California, birthplace of the new age. And brown and Black kids wouldn't be denied this healing. We would all sit under this Bodhi tree. We would snap back and forth through the portals availed to us. There are nightclubs that last the fraction of most lifetimes, let alone reincarnations. Mustache was special. But we didn't know it at the time.

Mustache held court in several downtown venues over the course of a decade. For me, Mustache came at a time marked by upheaval, a period of vulnerable adulthood butting up against restrictive episodes spurred by the stability-shattering of the 2008 recession. The frustrated energies echo today, and I am spirited back to a time of diminished job hours. But back then I could still turn heels and pump my fists to the beat in the necessary oblivions and escape hatches that Mustache offered me. It is these memories that kept the dream of nightlife alive when the pandemic foreclosed any remaining sense of futurity I had.

When you're younger, you excel at taking it all for granted. Or you don't realize how good this is because you timed your drugs correctly. Or you see the genealogy unfolding before your eyes and do the work of community making, no matter how much you end up hating each other. Or you're just trying to keep people from leaving the dance floor. Or you were always already borne from the necessary cliché that tomorrow isn't promised. Anyone with a generational membership doesn't realize that their points of contact with one another often transpire in these publics. That great love stories emerge here. That habits and vices do too. These are the sites that teach art while eschewing the prohibitive nature of respectability—it's where we are uninhibited by the vices of our choosing. The generation of queer Latinxs before me didn't have the freedom to be open in their exhibition of joy, the desiring of subjectivity, or the convergence of identities through song and dance. They were conditioned by gender. They drank through their social anxieties. They had to abide by the strict binaries, the rules of civility, familial and institutional legibility. Some veered toward homonormativity, relegating these furtive histories to one month a year. But I don't begrudge them. You actually have to plan to stay alive. Lives, not just history. Both deserve their own unearthing.

Acknowledgments

When your heart breaks and you pick up the pieces and put it back together, it sometimes takes shape as a book.

This book is born from the relational magic that shimmers from the anecdotal registers I have fallen in and out of over the course of the last seven years. It emerged from my travels and the escapades made possible by a host of institutions, workshops, parties, gatherings, and the gamut of intimate interactions. Such critical and pleasurable interventions never happen entirely alone but arise in the kindest of collaborations with friends, artists, colleagues, and fellow wanderers traversing the most troubled terrains. Thank you for the incredible experiences you have given me, which have buoyed me during the quietest, if not hardest, evenings alone at my desk.

Much of this labor was made possible by a generous award from the Andy Warhol Foundation Arts Writers Grant.

Thank you to Chris Fischbach for taking a chance on my work and for bringing me into the Coffee House family. Thank you to Lizzie Davis, Erika Stevens, Marit Swanson, Daley Farr, Kellie M. Hultgren, and Anitra Budd for your incredible guidance on this entire process. I raise a copita de mezcal to you all!

I thank Claudia LaRocca and Gordon Faylor for the guidance and editorial input on early versions of two essays, "Art in the Time of Art Washing" and "Baby Themme Anthems," originally published on *Open Space* in 2018. Thank you to Alex Espinoza and Boris Dralyuk for championing and publishing an early version of "Memories of the Skin: Shizu Saldamando's Portraits" in the *Los Angeles Review of Books* in 2018. I also thank Soham Patel for asking to publish "Do Migrants Dream of Blue Barrels" in the Spring 2020 issue of the *Georgia Review*. Thank you to Lucas Iberico Lozada for his incredibly generous feedback as my editor on an early version of "Behind the Barrier: Resisting the Border Wall Prototypes as Land Art" for *Popula*. I am in debt to Lou Cornum at *New Inquiry* for commissioning me to write about Laura Aguilar on the occasion of her passing. And my heartfelt thanks to the editors of *Rio Grande Review*, who published an early version of "Adobe in Pieces."

Thank you to Laura Aguilar, Lynn Ballen, Cecilia Brennan, San Cha, Jeanne Cordóva, rafa esparza, Timo Fahler, Sebastian Hernández, Xandra Ibarra, Joe Jiménez, Paulina S. Lara, Israel Lawrence, Rubén Martínez, Nacho Nava, Bradford Nordeen, Pau Pescador, Risa Puleo, Shizu Saldamando, Martín Sorrondeguy, Sandra K. Soto, Thea Q. Tagle, Alyn Tchurkin, and Michelle Téllez, for your inspirations cited throughout the book.

My additional thanks are also owed to my mentors in the University of Arizona MFA Creative Writing program, especially Chris Cokinos, Alison Deming, Ander Monson, and Aisha Sabatini Sloan, and Susan Briante, Farid Matuk, Manuel Muñoz, and Brandon Shimoda. A big, heartfelt set of thank-yous to my desert friends and cohort members for their immense warmth and generosities: Taneum Bambrick,

Samuel Rafael Barber, Paco Cantú, Sylvia A. Chan, Patrick Cline, Thomas Dai, Gabriel Dozal, Lee Anne Galloway, Danielle Geller, Rafa Gonzalez, Katie Gougelet, Ryan Kim, Lucy Kirkman, Natalie Lima, Claire Meuschke, Maddie Norris, Gabriel Palacios, Katerina Ivanov Prado, Michelle Repke, Josh Riedel, Dorian Rolston, Margo Steines, Kou Sugita, and Miranda Trimmier.

I thank my family of origin for their love and support, especially my mother, María Orbelina Gutiérrez, and my late father, José Javier Olvera Gutiérrez. Thank you to my siblings, Nina and Jaime.

Special thanks to my Los Angeles family of friends for their visionary love, guidance, and mentorship, especially Brent Armendinger, Ron Athey, Alice Bag, Anne Bray, Danielle Brazell, Tisa Bryant, Colin Campbell, Sam Cohen, Nikki Darling, Jennifer Doyle, Joseph Gallucci, Anji Gaspar-Milanovic, Brian Getnick, Brian Girgus, Myriam Gurba, Shoghig Halajian, Jen Hofer, Darin Klein, Sandra de la Loza, Rubén Martínez, Carolina Miranda, Alan Nakagawa, Nacho Nava, Wendy Ortiz, Shizu Saldamando, Selene Santiago, Gabie Strong, Karen Tongson, and Felix Solano Vargas.

My reserves of gratitude spill over for my friends and colleagues in the Southwest and beyond. Thank you to Rosa Alcalá, Laura Capelin, Natalie Díaz, Óscar Moisés Díaz, Angel Dominguez, Gwyn Fisher, Fernando A. Flores, Josh T. Franco, Cristina Rivera Garza & Saul Hernández Vargas, Marie Sarita Gaytán, Sarah Gzemski, Leticia Hernandez, Tim Johnston, Lazz Kinnamon, Leslie Martinez, Pete Mitchell, Caitlin Murray, Caitlin O'Hara, mónica teresa ortiz, Maryam Parhizkar, Grace Rosario Perkins, Ash Ponders, Sarah Schulman (who told me I should go get an MFA), Jeff Sirkin, Carmen Giménez Smith, Patrick Song, and Roberto Tejada.

I also want to honor the memories of José Esteban Muñoz, one of my early teachers of performance, politics, and genre promiscuity; and Toby Gutiérrez, my sweet pitbull mix who rode on many of my adventures throughout the Southwest and West Coast this last decade—thank you for being my copilot.

My love for and gratitude to Sandy Soto knows no bounds—thank you for bringing me to the desert. Te quiero chingos.

Coffee House Press began as a small letterpress operation in 1972 and has grown into an internationally renowned non-profit publisher of literary fiction, essay, poetry, and other work that doesn't fit neatly into genre categories.

Coffee House is both a publisher and an arts organization. Through our *Books in Action* program and publications, we've become interdisciplinary collaborators and incubators for new work and audience experiences. Our vision for the future is one where a publisher is a catalyst and connector.

LITERATURE
is not the same thing as
PUBLISHING

Funder Acknowledgments

Coffee House Press is an internationally renowned independent book publisher and arts nonprofit based in Minneapolis, MN; through its literary publications and Books in Action program, Coffee House acts as a catalyst and connector—between authors and readers, ideas and resources, creativity and community, inspiration and action.

Coffee House Press books are made possible through the generous support of grants and donations from corporations, state and federal grant programs, family foundations, and the many individuals who believe in the transformational power of literature. This activity is made possible by the voters of Minnesota through a Minnesota State Arts Board Operating Support grant, thanks to the legislative appropriation from the Arts and Cultural Heritage Fund. Coffee House also receives major operating support from the Amazon Literary Partnership, Jerome Foundation, McKnight Foundation, Target Foundation, and the National Endowment for the Arts (NEA). To find out more about how NEA grants impact individuals and communities, visit www.arts.gov.

Coffee House Press receives additional support from Bookmobile; Dorsey & Whitney LLP; Elmer L. & Eleanor J. Andersen Foundation; Fredrikson & Byron, P.A.; the Matching Grant Program Fund of the Minneapolis Foundation; Mr. Pancks' Fund in memory of Graham Kimpton; the Schwab Charitable Fund; and the U.S. Bank Foundation.

The Publisher's Circle of Coffee House Press

Publisher's Circle members make significant contributions to Coffee House Press's annual giving campaign. Understanding that a strong financial base is necessary for the press to meet the challenges and opportunities that arise each year, this group plays a crucial part in the success of Coffee House's mission.

Recent Publisher's Circle members include many anonymous donors, Patricia A. Beithon, Anitra Budd, Andrew Brantingham, Dave & Kelli Cloutier, Mary Ebert & Paul Stembler, Jocelyn Hale & Glenn Miller, the Rehael Fund-Roger Hale/Nor Hall of the Minneapolis Foundation, Randy Hartten & Ron Lotz, Dylan Hicks & Nina Hale, William Hardacker, Kenneth & Susan Kahn, Stephen & Isabel Keating, the Kenneth Koch Literary Estate, Cinda Kornblum, Jennifer Kwon Dobbs & Stefan Liess, the Lambert Family Foundation, the Lenfestey Family Foundation, Sarah Lutman & Rob Rudolph, the Carol & Aaron Mack Charitable Fund of the Minneapolis Foundation, Gillian McCain, Malcolm S. McDermid & Katie Windle, Mary & Malcolm McDermid, Daniel N. Smith III & Maureen Millea Smith, Peter Nelson & Jennifer Swenson, Enrique & Jennifer Olivarez, Alan Polsky, Robin Preble, Jeffrey Sugerman & Sarah Schultz, Nan G. Swid, Grant Wood, and Margaret Wurtele.

For more information about the Publisher's Circle and other ways to support Coffee House Press books, authors, and activities, please visit www.coffeehousepress.org/pages/donate or contact us at info@coffeehousepress.org.

Raquel Gutiérrez is an arts critic, writer, poet, and educator. Born and raised in Los Angeles, Gutiérrez credits the queer and feminist DIY, post-punk zine culture of the 1990s, plus Los Angeles County and Getty paid arts internships, for introducing her/them to the various vibrant art and music scenes and communities throughout Southern California. Gutiérrez is a 2021 recipient of the Rabkin Prize in Arts Journalism and a 2017 recipient of the Andy Warhol Foundation Arts Writers Grant. She is/They are faculty for Oregon State University–Cascades' Low Residency MFA in Creative Writing. Gutiérrez calls Tucson, Arizona, home.

Brown Neon was designed by
Bookmobile Design & Digital Publisher Services.
Text is set in Arno Pro.